THE
WRITING
BUSINESS

THE WRITING BUSINESS

Donald MacCampbell

CROWN PUBLISHERS, INC. NEW YORK

"Donald MacCampbell is one of the more rugged individualists in the agent field, and he likes to sell books that make money. He works hard, is successful. He's a defender of the author. He doesn't nit-pick; when he wants the deal he sees it through with dispatch. To him, a name writer is one who makes money. What makes MacCampbell unique among agents is that he is totally unpretentious. But he's tough and there are few mysteries in the business for him. I like his forthrightness."

WILLIAM TARG in *Indecent Pleasures*

© 1978 by Donald MacCampbell

This paperback edition published 1980.
Printed in the United States of America
Published simultaneously in Canada by
General Publishing Company Limited

Designed by Ruth Kolbert Smerechniak

Library of Congress Cataloging in Publication Data

MacCampbell, Donald.
    The writing business.

    1. Authorship. I. Title.
PN151.M27   808'.025   78–8397
ISBN: 0-517-532778 (cloth)
       0-517-542277 (paper)

10   9   8   7   6   5

Contents

Introduction

ALMOST ALL BOOKS ON WRITING HAVE ONE THING IN COMMON: they are egregiously dull. I have written a few of them myself, and I should know. For one thing, they are too serious. Even worse is their blind idealism. They try to give the impression that publishing is a gentlemanly profession with ethical standards much higher than those found in other occupations. It simply is not true. As I have tried to show in this book, it has among its conglomerate of agents, writers, publishers, and editors as many villains as heroes. It has men and women of dubious integrity from whom you would not think of buying a used car; it also has men and women whom you would trust with your dearest possessions, including the keys to your yacht and wine cellar.

At risk of vexing those who would prefer strictly nose-to-the-grindstone books about the trade of writing, I have tried in what follows to interlard factual information with subjective observations and even personal opinions. I am sure my dislike for Henry Miller's erotica will not nullify my statements concerning the proper way to prepare a manuscript any more than my remarks about publishers' dirty tricks will destroy a reader's faith in Publishers Row.

Perhaps the more innovative sections need some explanation. Part Four was designed to give the writer-reader a chance to examine some of the things that can go wrong with various types of material that an agent receives for marketing. I have tried to select only those office reports—not all of them written by me—which exemplify typical shortcomings: some remediable, some not. In Part Five I have presented a number of questions that arise repeatedly but which, while germane, do not invite answers which fit into the body of the book.

To establish a conversational style, I have allowed myself the use of the first person singular. There is a difference between *talking* to a reader and *lecturing*. I have chosen the former approach, with which I am more at home. However, to scotch any charge that the text is self-serving, I have carefully refrained from publicizing either the names of clients or my achievements as an agent. To that extent, at least, the work is objective—unlike the books of certain other ten percenters which have provided their authors with the opportunity to toot their own horns.

DONALD MacCAMPBELL
Stamford, Connecticut

ABOUT
WRITING

Short story and article writers
will find little to interest them in sections 3, 4, and 8.
The remaining sections of Part One can, I hope,
be read profitably by all who seek to earn a living with the pen.

Be Sure You Have Something to Sell

MUCH OF WHAT IS PUT ON PAPER TODAY IS UNPUBLISHABLE. IT IS for this reason that editors take such a dim view of unsolicited material. It has been estimated that the three top book publishers in the country receive an average of more than 3,000 over-the-transom manuscripts each year. Most of them go right back into the mail. You don't want yours to suffer this fate.

Some people regard writing as a form of therapy. Sidney Offit, who teaches at the New School in New York, has gone on record as believing they do not know the difference between creative work and self-pity. "Less than 5 percent have any sense of what a narrative is." The rest are men and women who have led tragic lives, suffered through the divorce mills, come up from wretched childhoods, endured great physical handicaps, and who feel the need to share their experiences with others. They sit down at a typewriter and start pecking away without having the slightest idea what a publishable work is about. Often they do not know how to indent for a paragraph. What they seem to be looking for is sympathy and understanding, rather than money.

There are the retired colonels who have spent the best part of their lives in the military and now turn to writing as a hobby. The captains, the majors, the generals all seem to find other leisure occupations. It is usually the colonels who fancy themselves latent literati and who find it hard to believe that agents and editors are not interested in them.

There are also the happy-go-lucky travelers who have discovered Europe or Asia or Africa and have kept careful diaries which they would love to turn into salable manuscripts. Almost all such writers are hopeless.

There are the Utopians and the reformers: the amateur sociologists, philosophers, financial experts, and lunch-table economists who believe they have hit upon viable solutions to the problems confronting the world. It never occurs to them that one must have credentials in order to be able to sell in specialized areas. Their books usually end up in the hands of vanity publishers who print a few copies for relatives and friends. (More about this later.)

Then, too, there are the young people whose experience with life has been limited to reading about it and who make a practice of aping their favorite authors. (I remember when I was in college I wanted to write like George Moore!) Narrative technique is indeed an important part of a novelist's tool kit, and it can be taught in the classroom. But what if a writer has nothing to say? Many of the thousands of unwanted manuscripts that are polluting the daily mail are intelligently prepared by young hopefuls but remind me of nothing so much as handsomely turned decanters that contain no wine.

Saddest of all are the untalented mercenaries who covet the vast sums of money that a few fortunate writers have made with their product. Perhaps they have heard of some middle-aged divorcée with a houseful of kids who has made a million dollars out of some mediocre erotic historical. Unfortunately this happens just often enough to inspire them to turn to the typewriter.

As manufacturing prices continue to soar and as the army of published writers continues to grow each year, life becomes more and more difficult for newcomers. An unknown name is always harder to sell, especially in the hardcover market where there is a noticeable shrinkage in the number of first novels. Roger Straus, of Farrar, Straus & Giroux, has stated somewhere that "if a novel sells only 3,500 copies the publisher loses only $7,000 to $10,000, provided he did not spend too much on advertising." This loss, of course, can be more than offset by a good reprint sale. A book acquired by a hardcover house for a $2,500 advance may fetch $100,000 or better for softcover rights. It does not usually happen. But it happens often enough to encourage new writers to gamble.

Every day my mail contains letters of inquiry from people who do not even bother to enclose self-addressed stamped envelopes.

Entire manuscripts are submitted, uninvited, and when returned without criticism frequently draw snotty letters.

Actually it is necessary to read only a few pages of a manuscript in order to gauge its potential. The very letter that accompanies the submission can be enough to turn one off, especially if it contains misspelled words, sloppy typing, bad grammar, and extravagant claims for the book's merit. Single-spaced copy, weird typography, colored ink, or pages produced entirely in capital letters, any one of these aberrations justifies putting the offering back into the mail.

First cousin to the *hopeless* manuscript is the *unlikely* one. Writers who have achieved some degree of success in pornography approach the legitimate market with meaningless credits. Everybody knows that the pornographers need master one thing: sex scenes capable of titillating morons. Style, plot, or characterization are irrelevant. Still they are distressed to learn that their credentials are worthless.

There is, however, one group of writers with whom I am inclined to be in sympathy: these are the people who have been turning out successful teleplays and who have decided to switch to novels. Having been preoccupied with writing nothing but dialogue, these would-be novelists find changing mediums does not come easily. You can spot these converts after reading a few pages of script in which the characters do nothing but talk. To switch from novels to teleplays presents fewer problems, and over the years I have lost my share of clients to Hollywood. But to move in the other direction is to court failure. As with the pornographer, the writer of teleplays fares no better in the New York market than does the rankest beginner, and often not so well.

These are some of the untouchables. Now you will want to know what you can write that is likely to sell. Stories and articles, even bad ones, can usually find a place *somewhere*: either among the newsstand periodicals or among the various "little" magazines that pay in free subscriptions. Books are a different matter.

Here are the kinds of books that are likely to sell:

FICTION

Novels that fit into distinct categories. Books of suspense, mystery, western, adventure, gothic, historical, romance, science fiction, and science fantasy. These books run upwards of 60,000 words, except for the historicals which run much longer. They are most easily written from a single point of view, first or third person. They require primarily sympathetic principal characters, although in the suspense novel the antihero is not uncommon. They require plenty of action, violent and otherwise; a varying degree of love interest; and some plot development, often an acceptable alternative to good writing.

General novels. These do not fall into any of the above categories and can be about almost anything. Slice-of-life stories, often autobiographical, are acceptable with strong writing and solid characterization. Formerly the general novel appeared only in hardcovers. Now you can find it in paperback. Like the fiction category referred to above, it can turn up in either format.

Biographical novels. Books about a real person but sufficiently well disguised to avoid lawsuits. Show business figures are frequently exploited in these stories, although it is possible to use characters drawn from history.

Autobiographical novels. These are more common than authors like to admit. Many so-called literary novelists draw largely from personal experience. Women are especially fond of putting themselves into their novels along with their relatives and friends. The amorphous nature of so much "literary" fiction is usually a giveaway. Sensitive writing is important, especially if the book is in the first person; otherwise it will read like a true-confession story.

Occupational novels. Books built around some unusual profession or trade. They are salable if they are made entertaining and if they leave the reader with a residue of vicarious experience: life as part of a deep-sea fishing fleet, as a lineman who climbs telegraph poles, as a sandhog who helps dig tunnels, as a pimp or a prostitute. These may be plotted or they may be written as slice-of-life fiction. Except for the more lurid occupations that are best suited for original paperback markets, these books usually have to make it in hardcovers.

Young people's novels. These run considerably shorter than novels for adults. Written about young characters engaged in youthful activities. You are not likely to get rich writing them, but so long as they are addressed to the right age levels they are a lot easier to write than adult fiction.

NONFICTION

Self-help and self-improvement books. These require modest credentials and generally display a level of writing that would never rate an A in a college course in composition. Even people who do not ordinarily buy books are interested in improving their looks or their health or their financial status. Many such books are spin-offs from the current best-seller lists.

Sexology books. These are perennial favorites among men and women whose minds are habitually focused below the waistline. In paperback, your credentials can be minimal. Many of the "quickies" you find on the newsstand consist of fabricated case studies designed to appeal to prurient interests. The hardcover books are usually by physicians or Ph.D.s and bring fat fees from reprinters who can stretch their sales into the millions. I sometimes wonder how so many babies ever managed to get born before all the handbooks telling readers how to make love!

Biographies. Painstakingly researched books that throw light upon the lives of famous men and women—often through the unearthing of long-lost letters. These are popular with hardcover publishers. There are also the superficial biographies of celebrities, written often without the knowledge or consent of the subjects, that come out as original paperbacks. Sports figures that make national headlines are also favorite targets of biographers.

How-to books. Written by those who know how to plant gardens, how to play tennis, how to embroider—the possibilities are endless and the necessary credentials are of a varying degree of importance, depending upon the fastidiousness of the publisher. There are dozens of books on how to write, most of them turned out by people who have never learned. This makes me suspicious of how-to books in other areas. If you are interested in doing one of these, you must not be discouraged to find a number of them already listed on subject index cards in your public library. How-to books are what publishers call stable perennials: with periodic updating they can go on forever, although they seldom make their authors much money.

Specialized subjects. These require an authority in the field and are not for the layman to produce. Economics, religion, sociology, criminology, biology, medicine, psychology, law—these are a few of the areas to avoid. Who you are is deemed almost as important as what you have to say.

Cookbooks. These are usually written by people with newspaper or magazine affiliations and therefore a following.

Young people's nonfiction. Books in any specialized area. These

6

are shorter and easier to read, and their authors need not have the high degree of standing in their field that is required in the adult market.

As the intended readership gets younger, careful attention must be paid to age groups. The authentic *juvenile*, and here I am thinking of the book slanted for preteen children, looks easier to write than it is. Teachers at primary and grammar school levels are best qualified to produce these books, although some perceptive parents number among the authors. Illustrations now become as important a part of the package as the editorial material. My advice to you about writing juvenile fiction or nonfiction is to forget it if you aspire to write for adults; it will do your style more harm than good.

Of course there are many other kinds of books. Here I have listed only the categories that are likely to interest you. Do a thoughtful, competent job in any of these areas and you will have something to sell.

Concerning the Manuscript

HOW YOU TACKLE THE PRELIMINARY DRAFTS OF YOUR MANUSCRIPT is of no importance to anyone but yourself. Some writers work on the typewriter exclusively, editing, expanding, deleting copy. Others like to dictate and turn over their tapes to professional typists. Still others prefer to do a first draft in longhand and then edit it as they put it through the machine. All that matters is that the version that goes to market has a professional appearance. To achieve this effect, the following points should be of some assistance:

First select a heavy paper. Choose one which does not permit type to show through. Onionskin, except for carbon copies, is no good. Paper that is so cheap that it will not stand up under erasures is a waste of money. Needless to say, the paper must be white.

It is not necessary to invest in rag content for the purpose of impressing editors. Paper that comes in folders is quite suitable; just be sure it has sufficient body. Avoid legal length, and do not use the kind with holes for binders.

Be sure your manuscript is double-spaced. If you have ever worked in an editorial office, you will know why this is essential. Not only is single-spaced copy difficult to read, but it is difficult to edit. There must always be space between the lines where the editor can make any necessary corrections and changes. No matter how excellent a book property may be, it is not likely to get a reading if single-spaced.

Another thing to consider is margining. Leave at least a one-and-one-half-inch margin on all sides of the manuscript. Margins are not only agreeable to the eye but they also serve a very practical purpose. Frequently an editor will want to make comments in the margins, or the copy editor will want to give instructions to the printer.

Take care in selecting a ribbon. Be sure it is in good condition. Beware of those red and blue ribbons that sometimes produce red tails on certain letters when they are supposed to be all blue. A one-color black ribbon is safest to use. And do not keep it in the machine so long that the typeface begins to fade and makes reading difficult.

I remember unearthing a script in one of the Atlantic Monthly Press contests that was typed in several colors. The letters were a dark purple with green underlinings for certain words, and the chapter headings were also in green. If this writer had used white paper the reading would have been difficult enough, but the paper was a creamy yellow. Naturally, the manuscript was returned unread.

Any conventional typeface is acceptable. Never use one that looks like handwriting. Do not decide to make your copy more legible by preparing it in capital letters. When the paper stops showing between the *o*'s and the *d*'s and the *g*'s, it is time to clean the letters. Kits are available for this purpose.

Start the first page halfway down the sheet. Then center the chapter title, if you have one, and type it in capital letters. At the upper left-hand corner of this first page be sure to type your name and address or the address of your agent. At the upper right-hand corner it is a good idea to type the approximate word length.

To number pages, center the number in the bottom margin and carry through consecutively. Do not begin renumbering at the start of each new chapter as writers have been known to do. Also, it is a good idea *not* to put the title of the work on every page in case the title has to be changed.

Always retain a carbon or a Xerox of everything you put in the mail. Manuscripts can be lost or misplaced. A commuting editor who takes your manuscript home to read may leave it in the bar car. Isolated pages may get mixed in with another manuscript lying next to it on an editor's desk. A substitute mailman may deliver it to the wrong address, and the receiver may go off on vacation and forget to give it back.

Proofread the copy. So much for the mechanics of manuscript preparation. Before surrounding it with cardboard and putting it into the mailbox, go over the copy with a fine-tooth-comb.

Writers are notoriously bad spellers and are often careless about inversions, word omissions, and syntax. While publishers pay copy editors to attend to these things, they have become expensive; I have known writers to be dropped on their heads for failure to present reasonably clean manuscripts. It is a mistake to count too heavily upon outside assistance. Accuracy is a habit worth cultivating.

Keep your manuscript in excellent condition. If you are doing your own marketing, watch closely for signs of deterioration. Wrinkled, coffee-stained pages are telltale evidence that your work has been making the rounds. It is always a good idea to give editors the impression they are getting the first look.

Never send out a carbon copy or a Xeroxed copy without an adequate explanation. Even though chances are that the editors will not believe that the original has been lost, chewed up by the family dog, or torn to pieces by an obstreperous young offspring, at least you will have offered apologies. A Xeroxed copy always indicates to me that the manuscript is being offered elsewhere simultaneously; when I receive one, I always ask to see the original. No agent enjoys being in a writer's shopping bag! No editor will take warmly to Xeroxed material unless it has been made clear in advance that the work is being auctioned. (And if it is being auctioned, it had better be good!)

When sending out a manuscript direct to a publisher, it is wise to address the editor by name. This is a mere formality, and in no way does it assure you of a personal reading by the person you send it to. Be careful not to address your envelope to a deceased editor or to one who has been sacked, for this shows at once that you have not been invited to submit but have picked the name off a market list that is out-of-date.

Always enclose a self-addressed envelope regardless of who is being asked to read your manuscript. It is better to send actual postage than a check; otherwise this small amount will have to go through bookkeeping. (In my agency checks are immediately returned, not because there is a danger of their bouncing but because they are a nuisance to handle.)

Manuscripts may be sent "Special Fourth Class Manuscript Rate." This is the least expensive way of sending them through the mail. If you must send them registered, do not be so bold as to suggest that they be returned in like manner, for it is not going to happen. This requires a special trip to the post office and usually involves standing in line. And who do you think you are anyway?

3

Today's Marketplace

TODAY THERE ARE FOUR OUTLETS FOR WRITERS WHEREAS A few decades ago there were only two: *magazines* and *hardcover books*. The forties saw the introduction of *mass-market paperbacks*, which began as reprint operations and later branched out into originals. Then came *oversized* or *trade paperbacks*, a format that hardcover publishers had all to themselves until recently when the mass-market firms decided to enter into competition.

Magazines have lost much of their readership to television, and it is not surprising to find *TV Guide* outstripping most of its newsstand rivals in circulation. Advertisers have also defected in great numbers, resulting in the collapse and demise of some of the nation's big-name periodicals. With magazine fiction unable to compete with the numerous dramatic entries that turn up on the idiot box, it is not surprising that the short story and the once-popular serial have virtually disappeared. Free-lance magazine writers who used to earn a precarious living writing fiction now grind out articles on a multitude of subjects: sports, travel, gardening, household maintenance, self-help, and self-improvement being among the most popular.

If you are a periodical writer you will probably never succeed in making a decent living, even if you specialize and achieve recognition in a particular area. Fees are not what they were in the days of *Colliers, American,* and the *Saturday Evening Post,* when vast sums were paid for material and writers were sent all over the world on special assignments. Free lancers today have to work much harder, have to turn out more copy, and accept more modest remuneration. Specialists—men and women with solid credentials—may still collect as much from an article as from a hardcover or trade paperback. But can they sell enough of these to the few good markets to make anything like a living?

Hardcover publishing is often subsidized by book clubs and paperback reprinters. Without subsidiary revenue, many could not survive. By putting out a portion of each season's list in trade-paperback format they can save on guarantees and also on royalties. But in a way they are competing with themselves. If, for example, they put out a book on gardening that sells in "paper" for $3.95, they can usually dismiss any hopes for future sales of a hardcover book on the same subject they may still have in print. If they have a $20 book on the subject of electricity and magnetic force and a competitor has the same material available in a trade paperback for $5, the $20 item is going to be clobbered in the bookstores.

All this has left booksellers in a quandary. Should they do what is logical and put all books in the two formats that deal with the same subject in one place and thus invite buyers to opt for the less expensive property? Should they isolate the trade paperback, perhaps limit their orders substantially, in an effort to push the more expensive hardcover titles and risk losing a sale altogether?

You will probably agree that too many books are being published, some of them spin-offs and imitations of established best-sellers. Many paperback publishers feel obliged to put out X number of titles each season and to fill up with inferior products where necessary. This, of course, gives the marginal writer a break, but it does not increase the publisher's reputation or, necessarily, his margin of profit.

The reading public has become much more sophisticated in recent years and also much wiser. Hardcover fiction is difficult to sell, especially if the author is relatively unknown. Booksellers do not want to load up on fillers. They tend to siphon off the top three or four titles on a publisher's list and ignore unknown names—especially first novelists. For this reason publishers frequently have to count on subsidiary revenue to bail out first novels and do not count on bookstore sales. Also, a smart reader of fiction knows that within a year after the hardcover publication of a novel, even a best-seller, the work is going to be available on a paperback rack.

It is in the area of nonfiction that the hardcover publisher does best in the bookstores. Most nonfiction becomes dated more slowly and may be kept in print for years before having to be remaindered. There is usually nothing deader than last season's hardcover edition of a novel, even if it bears the name of an established author. Since it is the nonfiction book that is usually put into an oversized-paperback edition—either simultaneously or at a later date—many observers of the publishing scene are inclined to wonder if such editions are as good for the publishers as for the bookstore customers who shy away from inflated hardcover prices.

As a writer you can let the publishers worry about these problems, and you can console yourself with the knowledge that the oversized or trade paperback offers you a market in between the mass paperbacks and the hardcovers. Many types of non-fiction make attractive original oversized paperbacks: definitive studies of limited appeal; handbooks on gardening; cookbooks; business books; books in the area of religion, education, or economics; almanacs; guidebooks; how-to and self-improvement books; and many others. These usually retail for under $5, whereas a hardcover book would have to cost twice as much and the publisher would have to think twice as hard before offering you a contract. *Literary Market Place*, which I will have occasion to mention more than once in this book, is the most reliable source of information if you are looking for an oversized-paperback market. There are firms that publish only in this attractive format, thereby furnishing the public with works that are easy to read and that are printed on quality paper—making them worth storing on a bookshelf.

Until recently, almost all trade paperbacks featured nonfiction alone. Now the mass-market operators are starting to "pre-publish" fiction by established name authors in the larger format, charging roughly twice what they will charge at a later date for the regulation-size paperback. Avon was the first to experiment, using one of its popular romance writers and testing the market in Hawaii before exploring it on the mainland. Attractive dumps, or bins, are beginning to appear alongside the usual racks in supermarkets and chain stores; however, it will probably be several years before the success or failure of this new trend can be determined for certain. It may be even longer before the marketing of original paperback fiction by lesser known authors will be attempted. For the present, what you have is a new development, perhaps the most important in years. With trade paperbacks already showing the most gratifying expansion among the four formats, there is reason for optimism at this time.

The mass-market paperback, which has been accepting original material ever since Fawcett started Gold Medal Books back in 1950, is now and will continue to be the writer's best friend. Since the books are manufactured as inexpensively as possible and designed to be thrown away after reading, it is not necessary to fill them with deathless prose. Darwin's law of the survival of the fittest is certain to work effectively in paperback publishing, and as inflation increases and pushes retail prices higher and higher you will find the weaker imprints being forced off the market. Several have already been saved by merging with stronger companies intent upon upgrading their output.

Trade paperbacks will probably always favor nonfiction material, for which they are so ideally suited. Mass-market paperbacks, with few exceptions, have always favored fiction and will continue to do so, since once a novel has been read it is usually ready to be disposed of. When I think how gingerly Fawcett raised the price of its Gold Medal Books from 25¢ to 35¢ back in the fifties, I am appalled at the recent increases which have many paperback novels selling over the $2 mark. By the time you read this the $1.25 book will probably be nonexistent, since costs all along the line have been pushing prices upward.

There is a serious danger inherent in these increases. The unknown, the marginal novelist, the writer who finds it difficult to sustain interest in the longer lengths that are now favored, may live to see the time when the quality of their product does not live up to even the lowest retail price of a mass-paperback book. Editors are well aware of a publisher's inability to sell slum fiction at Park Avenue rates. It is something to bear in mind.

4

Choosing a Publisher

IF YOU WORK THROUGH AN AGENT, THIS CHAPTER IS NOT FOR YOU. However, if you attempt to do your own selling, you will have to make a careful study of the field. A good place to start is to familiarize yourself with the contents of the following two publications. Having done this, you can write for individual catalogs and ask to be put on mailing lists for special announcements.

Literary Market Place, published once a year, contains the names and addresses of all legitimate firms, along with the makeup of their staffs. Under each listing is information concerning the firm's particular fields of activity. One copy of *LMP* is more valuable than a year's subscription to any writer's magazine.

Publishers Weekly is another good investment on the part of an unagented writer. This contains the latest gossip in the trade, announcements about the newest books, reviews of forthcoming releases, and advertisements of books already on sale. Twice a year subscribers are treated to giant issues in which publishers frequently advertise a complete list of their latest offerings.

A new writer does not usually choose a publisher. The publisher is more likely to do the choosing. There may be numerous rejections to contend with once your manuscript has begun making the rounds, and the firm that finally accepts it may not be among your preferred houses.

There was a time not long ago when multiple submissions were considered unethical. A writer was expected to send a manuscript, or the outline of a proposed project, to only one firm at a time. Since it may take from several weeks to several months to get a decision, single submissions do not really make sense; nevertheless, a number of old-line publishers still require them.

What you must do, when you have something that you feel is ready to sell, is write to a number of firms that might be interested in your kind of material and inquire whether or not they will consider unagented submissions and, if so, whether or not *multiple* submissions are agreeable. Of course, if you want to be sneaky about it, and if you can afford the expense of having several top copies of a project prepared, you can make your multiple submissions to firms willing to consider your work and they need know nothing about it. Let your conscience be your guide. But in any event be sure to enclose a self-addressed stamped envelope with your inquiry in order to be reasonably certain of receiving a reply.

Having picked out a few publishing houses that seem to favor your type of product, and having been given the green light by more than one, how do you now proceed? This is difficult to answer, for publishing is a complex business and things are not always what they seem. The firm that makes those beautiful books you see in the bookstores may be chintzy about advances. Another firm that does a lot of advertising in the *New York Times Book Review* may have a weak rights department. If you favor a small publisher, it is possible he may have a cash flow problem and may have to sell off your subsidiary rights for peanuts. Pick a firm that puts out a flock of best-sellers and you may find yourself being used as filler on an impressive list of big names. Select one with a small and undistinguished roll of authors and this may be the one that will keep your book in print the longest and decide not to remainder it after only a few months.

Every publisher is different; every contract is different. You may think you have an ideal offer, possibly from the firm you put at the top of your list. So you sign a contract only to discover later that there is no provision for publication within a certain date and that the portion of your advance that you agreed to accept on publication may be bottled up for several years.

It is quite possible that the publisher who insists upon your making revisions before signing you up will do a better selling job than the one who gives you a fast contract and lets you talk him out of alterations. The publisher who insists upon seeing a complete manuscript may be in a position to earn you twice as much money as the one who, desperate for material, signs you on the basis of an outline alone.

Theoretically, a writers' club that admits only established writers—if such a club exists—should be able to disseminate enough information about good and bad publishers to keep its members informed. But as writers like to exaggerate and to vent their personal antipathies, it is unlikely that rumor and ugly gossip could ever be distinguished from fact. Most writers' groups, including the Authors' Guild, are open to anybody who has somehow managed to get out a book and is willing to cough up the dues.

Booksellers are most likely to have reliable firsthand information about publishers, since they handle their product and are familiar with their personnel. Librarians are another source of information; ask them which publishers they hold in highest esteem and why.

The choice between a large house and a small one is a matter of individual preference. Some writers are temperamentally better suited to a small organization that is likely to give them personal attention. Others, who like to brush shoulders with famous names, may be happier in a large establishment. It is a question of whether you prefer being a big fish in a small pond or part of a list the size of a small-town telephone directory.

Nowadays publishers large and small are being gobbled up by conglomerates. The privately owned companies are becoming harder to find in *Literary Market Place*. Some of the conglomerations seem to make sense, as when a motion picture or a large television operation takes on a New York publisher and opens up new vistas for writers. When a hardcover firm absorbs a paperback reprinter, this too augurs well for its authors, but when the merger is later taken over by a conglomerate composed of alien corporate interests the advantages are doubtful.

How to choose a publisher if you are given the opportunity to do so? First go through all the motions I have indicated. Then cross your fingers and pray!

5

Publishers' Contracts

THE FACT THAT THERE IS NO SUCH THING AS A STANDARD CON-tract makes negotiating a tricky business. Advances, which are of primary importance to most writers, bear no relation whatever to their financial needs. Length of product, track record, likely reception by book clubs, reprint houses, and reading public, the condition of the publisher's cash flow—these are matters that determine the amount of money you can expect up front.

Editors are always trying to tell writers that advances are not that important. Do not buy such nonsense. Semiannual royalty statements are notorious for their goose eggs. Whether you write hardbacks or paperbacks, you must be prepared for the worst. The book that takes off and enjoys a runaway sale, and gets discussed in the *New York Times* for all writers to drool over, is the exception. You, or your agent if you have one, must try to obtain an advance that is reasonable to you and reasonable to the publisher. The Authors' Guild has recently estimated that fully 40 percent of all books published earn nothing over the advance, which I feel to be a conservative estimate. They also estimate that 40 percent of the authors receive $5,000 or less prior to publication. When you consider that reprint publishers have paid over $3,000,000 for acquisitions, a $5,000 advance seems pathetically inadequate. Yet a hardcover firm can lose money on even this small an investment.

In all fairness it must be said that there *are* good publishers who are reluctant to hand out large sums of money in advance and who nevertheless get by with their policy because of exceptionally strong rights departments. But what happens with such firms is that lesser known writers are simply carried along for the ride while the bulk of the company's energy is devoted to securing enormous sums for the subsidiary rights to books by the "big names."

Advances are normally paid in two or three installments. If a finished manuscript is unacceptable and the publisher decides to write off the project, then the writer, especially if a valuable account, may simply be invited to return the money if the work is sold elsewhere. Nowadays, however, a number of publishers' contracts stipulate that *all* monies paid down must be refunded if the work proves to be unacceptable. If the amount is large enough, the publisher may go all the way to court in an effort to recover.

When you get into the area of big advances—and here I mean advances in six figures—a publisher will have managed to get precommitments on the part of subsidiary markets; much, if not all, of the hardcover advance in such instances will come out of such revenue. You will have to look far and wide to find a hardcover publisher willing to shell out a six-figure advance to an author who has no established track record of best-sellers unless there is some backstage arrangement which the author may know nothing about.

I have always been surprised at the way publishers agree to pay large advances on unwritten projects they could in all likelihood latch onto with inexpensive options, much the way movie producers operate. This would certainly minimize their gamble. A few publishers, Doubleday being one, do make it a practice to take options, and to me this makes a lot of sense. A writer submits an outline or a table of contents; the publisher agrees, for a nominal fee, to take an option on the work, one that will give him a look at a couple of sample chapters at the very least. If satisfied with the sample, he then secures the acquisition by issuing a regular contract and providing a full advance. This was the way *Jaws* came into being, and I am sure the author of this blockbuster novel has no regrets about the arrangement.

Advances paid to writers who do their own selling are usually a fraction of what they would be if the contracts were negotiated through an agent. When I read that a publisher does not like to negotiate directly with writers, I know that what he really means is he hates the thought of maintaining a staff large enough to dispose of a slush pile. If he can get hold of *publishable* writers, not represented by agents, he is delighted. Think of the money to be saved by doling out chintzy advances, grabbing unfair percentages of translation, first serial, and motion picture rights. (I once saw a top-ranked publisher's contract that granted the publisher 50 percent of all subsidiary revenue!)

Sometimes an agent gets to see some of the shameful contracts offered directly to naive writers, a fact that publishers do not count on. I have seen contracts providing for no advance at all, for royalties based on the wholesale rather than the retail price of the book, even for an outright sale of the property with no royalty payment. I suppose this might come under the heading of "dirty tricks," but I prefer to think of it as author stupidity.

Pick up a copy of *Publishers Weekly* and you will see the titles of hundreds upon hundreds of new books published each year. A sizable number of these are unagented since they are in areas not likely to produce enough commission to interest a middleman; this leaves many writers open to victimization.

From time to time I am approached by these unagented writers and am shown, by way of credentials, Xeroxed copies of their contracts. The no-advance deals are the ones that have always irked me most, and I once called an editor who had issued a no-advance contract and asked him why. "We don't pay advances on this type of book," I was told quite bluntly. "We don't have to. We have more writers willing to take their chances on sales than you would like to believe." I was astounded. I received a similar jolt some years ago when I queried another top publisher on one of their pay-on-wholesale contracts which had fallen into my hands. "It helps defray the cost of the pictures," I was told.

Publishers like to issue long contracts with numerous superfluous clauses when an adequate contract can usually be printed on the two sides of one sheet of paper. Many of the printed clauses can be accepted without suspicion. The parts that are typed in are all negotiable and must be carefully examined:

Territorial coverage. Publishers *lease* North American, English language, or world publishing rights. (They seldom actually *buy* them.)

Delivery. The contract should stipulate a delivery date, and it is a good idea to ascertain in advance if it is going to be possible to get an extension if more time is needed.

Publication. A contract should state an outside date for putting the book on the market; it should provide for termination in the event the work is not published by that time.

Subsidiary rights. Second serial, book club, and reprint rights are usually sold on a fifty-fifty basis; publishers ask for, but do not always get, 10 percent of first serial and from 10 to 50 percent of translation, motion picture, television, and dramatic rights. It is in this area that most horse-trading takes place.

Sliding scale. For a hardcover work, the writer generally gets 10 percent on the first 5,000 copies sold, 12.5 percent on the next 5,000, and 15 percent thereafter. However, everything over the initial 10 percent is negotiable, and established writers often start at 15 percent. Mass paperback royalties run from 6 up to 10 percent, the graduated scale starting at between 150,000 copies sold to 250,000. Trade paperback royalties vary but are much lower.

Options. A good clause to eliminate if possible. If the publisher insists upon an option, it should be on one particular book and "on terms to be arranged"; never allow identical terms to apply to any other book unless the original terms happen to impress you as being fantastic.

Chargeable expenses. These are negotiable, but expect to pay for proof corrections over a specified figure, for indexing, and often for illustrations.

Termination. Contracts issued by reputable publishers can usually be terminated by the author once a book is out-of-print and not slated to be reissued. Written request for termination is acted upon in different ways. A contract may commit the publisher to declare, within X number of days, an intention to put out a new edition by a stipulated date once the request has been received. Many contracts provide for termination after the expiration of a specified number of years if the publisher feels there is not sufficient demand for the work to keep it in print, or if it is out-of-print in all editions. All contracts should provide for termination if the publisher defaults in the delivery of semiannual statements or in making payments as provided in such contracts, but following written notification of such default, a publisher is entitled to at least thirty days in which to honor the agreement. Each publisher, hardcover or paperback, offers different conditions for termination; but even if a contract reads "for the duration of copyright," there should be provision for recovering rights once the active life of a property no longer exists.

6

Be Your Own Press Agent

ONE OF THE MOST IMPORTANT THINGS FOR YOU TO KNOW AT THE outset of a writing career is the part that promotion plays in determining success or failure. A publisher cannot do it all. Publishers' publicity departments are notoriously ineffective: not because they do not try, but because a publicity department has too many books to promote at any one time, so that not enough attention can be devoted to any one unless it be by a big name author whose work is likely to become a best-seller.

We live in a publicity-mad society. Shyness, modesty, humility—good old-fashioned virtues—are no longer meaningful and can be counterproductive. You must know the value of autographing parties, talk shows, lecture engagements, and press conferences. You must accept the fact that a five-minute interview between commercials on the *Today* show is going to sell more copies of a book than a full-page advertisement in the *New York Times*.

Of course if you are unknown, and have only a sale or two to your credit, your promotional efforts will, of necessity, be more subtle. Television talk shows will have no part of you. Women's clubs will be reluctant to part with their minimum $50 fees. Columnists will grant you nary a line. What then?

There are still possibilities: letter columns in big-city newspapers, radio call-in shows, citizen's band radio, contributions to those small periodicals that pay in free subscriptions, flattering notes to book reviewers (flattery is always a useful weapon), and finally, any connection you may have with some writer of importance: a neighbor, a sixth cousin, or a classmate from high school or college. Maybe you know some interesting fact about the person that the press does not and might like to publicize: something interesting but not scandalous. For example, you may know a prominent author who has invented a new cocktail. Or you may have overheard a superstitious publisher at a party confess that he never puts a book out on Friday the thirteenth. Maybe you have learned that an editor friend writes novels under a pen name which happens to be his real name spelled backwards. This is the harmless kind of fluff that columnists feed on. (But never send the same item to more than one columnist, and be sure to mark it *exclusive.*)

Make it a firm policy to avoid useless companions—at least until you can afford them. Never get involved with writers' groups, for you will find the members much too preoccupied with themselves to be of any value. If you must be a joiner, better to join the Elks or the Lions or the Rotarians; or take up collection in church where you may run into successful elderly businessmen— Babbits though they may be—who are in a position to offer a hand. Who knows? You may even run into a PR person who can give you a shove in the right direction.

The one thing you must never do is try to promote your cause aggressively with an editor or agent who has shown an interest in your work. Take my word for it, this can be disastrous. Any time I receive a manuscript from a pompous unknown who calls up long distance to tell me how great it is and how much money it is going to earn for all concerned, including the movie producer, I know it is something to be put in a trash can.

Now it is true that a good-looking lady writer, whether established or not, can charm a "receptive" editor into taking a special interest in her career. Most heterosexual editors I know, and even a few oversexed publishers, are vulnerable to pulchritude—probably because there is so little of it in the creative sphere. As a lady writer once remarked to me over cocktails, "The best place to discuss terms with an editor is in bed after a couple of double martinis."

Okay, you are not a good-looking lady writer. Let us assume you already have latched on to an agent. What then? You must not sit back and expect this agent to do all the necessary legwork. Most successful authors make the editorial rounds periodically and frequently come up with deals on their own. It happens every day. Some writers are simply better hucksters than their representatives. I have had clients successfully sell projects that I have turned down, and each time it has happened I have facetiously—but with ill-concealed embarrassment—suggested they go into the business.

Clients who are good salespeople and natural PR types can substantially increase their income by developing personal contacts in the trade. You will find that secure agents do not resent this so long as they pick up their 10 percent. What they will resent, of course, is any attempt you may make to put your fingers into a pie they have been baking.

We move in the shadow of Madison Avenue. Nothing is what it seems and little that one reads is believable. No writer is as good as his promoters would like you to think. But make no mistake about it, this phoniness has its uses in marketing a product. For proof one has only to read a publisher's jacket blurb, or the nonsense he prints in his advertisements, to see how minimal is the relationship between the quality of a literary property and the description given the public: "The greatest historical since *Gone With the Wind*"; "If you loved *War and Peace*, you will love this novel"; "The most earthy love story since Adam and Eve"; and so on *ad nauseam*.

One blatant example of this phony activity is a large paperback house that went so far as to establish a policy of printing its own best-seller list composed of books it has on sale. Once, when I found one of my own client's turkeys listed, I asked the editor how come the book's success was not reflected in the royalty statement. "Ignore it," I was told. "It's just a way we have of playing up books that have bombed—the idea being to recoup a bad investment."

I suspect that if any current product, be it an automobile, a vacuum cleaner, or whatever, were to be honestly described, there would be few takers. Books are no exception. You just cannot permit them to come barefaced into being. They must be cosmetized, bewigged, perfumed, given padding where needed for the sake of appearance. Having accomplished this much, a publisher may feel he has performed his duty. At this point a clever writer should go to work.

To begin with, I suggest that you spend a part of each day writing letters. Famous writers enjoy receiving fan mail and are hurt when they do not get any. Most of them are quite approachable, drunk or sober. (The ones, like Salinger, who sequester themselves from the public, are rare.) It is a pretty neat trick to become a pen pal of an established author or two who may be in a position to help you. Flattery, I repeat, is a handy weapon, and successful authors are no different from other people in their desire to be admired. Many of them are married to nags who resent the long hours their mates spend at the typewriter, and they will invariably suck up like a vacuum cleaner any bits of adulation from the outside.

Years ago, in my spare time, I edited a little magazine called *The Writer*. I was amazed to find how easy it was to secure short autobiographical pieces from big name novelists for what amounted to lunch money—and in those days lunches were inexpensive. I discovered that writers enjoy scribbling about themselves and explaining how they go about their business.

In my time I have seen editors come and go, publishers rise and fall. I have seen how best-sellers are manufactured, often out of offal. Today success smiles on those with the most brass and ingenuity and not necessarily the most talent. Without the tireless efforts of her aggressive husband, the novels of Jacqueline Susann—titles of which I have seen stamped in white on the very pavements of New York—might have passed unheralded. (Actually she was a damn good writer.) Without their ubiquitous public appearances such exhibitionists as Norman Mailer, John Kenneth Galbraith, and Truman Capote might be lost in the crowd.

Modesty is the enemy of talent.

7

The Model Writer

THE PRIVILEGE OF THROWING YOUR WEIGHT AROUND IS IN DIRECT ratio to your reputation as a writer. No agent or editor is going to put up with a hardhead who does not make money for all concerned. Exuberance is one thing, but belligerence is something else. I cannot tell you how many young and talented writers have had doors closed to them because they have been too difficult. Male writers are by far the worst offenders. Even women's libbers cannot match them for arrogance.

Let me give you an imaginary portrait of the model writer. Test yourself and see how many of these qualities you possess and where you are most likely to fall short.

Talent. You can be a pussycat, but if you have nothing to sell who needs you? You may charm a member of the opposite sex into wanting to help you, but in the end you must have something more to offer than good vibes.

Flexibility. Can you accept constructive criticism? No editor or agent gets extra fees for telling you where you are making mistakes, and neither is under any obligation to nurse a sick product. Even if you should disagree with the criticism, be careful not to resent it.

Graciousness. If your manuscript is returned for revision, and especially if you are given to believe the revision may lead to a contract, be appreciative. When you receive a check write a thank-you letter, even though you know the money does not come out of the editor's or the agent's own pocket. Polite gestures of this kind cost no more than a telephone call or a postage stamp, and they make good impressions.

Dependability. You faithfully meet the delivery date specified in your contract—deadlines are taken seriously. If, for some unavoidable reason, a delivery threatens to be late, you request an extension. Such a request is seldom refused in the face of an emergency.

Loyalty. Once you are firmly established in your career you may need an agent like a hole in the head, but you do not walk off just to save the 10 percent. If you have a publisher who has worked hard to build your name, you do not allow yourself to be lured away by an aggressive competitor who offers a slightly larger advance. Loyalty demands that you at least give the old firm an opportunity to match any new offer.

Temperance. The model writer has a minimum of bad personal habits, such as an excessive fondness for liquor, a penchant for borrowing money, an inclination to gamble away earnings, or a tendency to get into domestic difficulties.

Do such writers actually exist? I have encountered a few. Unfortunately they are like the "good": they usually die very young.

8

The Dangers
of Collaboration

YOU SHOULD NEVER TEAM UP WITH ANOTHER WRITER, NOT EVEN IF
you are man and wife, unless you know deep down it would be
impossible for you to cut it alone. This admonition does not apply
to ghostwriters who make it possible for nonwriters with
something to say to break into print. I am thinking rather of those
cozy relationships between friends, relatives, neighbors, or
classmates that result in coproduction of fiction—yes, and also of
nonfiction—manuscripts.

It is true that some collaborations seem to work. Not too long
ago the publishing business was treated to a novel entitled *Naked
Came the Stranger* which actually was the work of several newspaper men, each of whom had a fling at a chapter or two; the book,
while containing some amusing scenes, achieved an early demise,
and to the best of my knowledge the collaborators were never
heard from again. Most writing teams are made up of two members who form a kind of partnership and agree in advance
upon the contribution each intends to make.

Literary partnerships, of course, are nothing new. I've always
thought of Addison and Steele as an eighteenth-century writing
team, but actually they were no more than intimate friends who
wrote separately for the *Spectator*, a publication which appeared
daily, sold for twopence, and went into 555 issues. Much of Addison's best writing appeared in the *Spectator*, although Steele provided most of the material and put his own imprimatur upon
all that he wrote.

I suppose a model for collaborators was the team of Beaumont and Fletcher. Lowell, in his lectures on old English dramatists, wrote: "They are as inseparately linked together as Castor and Pollux. Their beams are so indissolubly mingled that it is vain to attempt any division of them that shall assign to each his rightful share." They were unique in that their collaboration was fairly uncommon among the lesser Elizabethan dramatists at this time, when managers parceled out single acts, or even scenes, among two or three different playwrights in order to achieve a multi-talented combination.

In modern times there was a highly successful fiction team of Nordhoff and Hall, whose *Mutiny on the Bounty* topped the best-seller lists over a period of many months. Both became darlings of the critics, gained stature as *literary* authors as opposed to commercial hacks, and were forgiven for making a considerable amount of money. They were the exception to the rule, just as, at a much lower literary level, the team of writers known as Ellery Queen managed to hold together successfully over a long period of years.

From personal observation and experience I will venture to estimate the chances of your forming a successful writing team at one in ten. There are too many pitfalls along the way. Consider a few:

These days with one out of every three marriages ending in divorce, a team composed of man and wife has no reason to feel secure. Think of all the domestic skirmishes that can injure and disable a relationship! It seems to me, if one must enter a literary partnership, the less one member knows about the private life and problems of the other the better its chances of succeeding. I would never consider representing a man-and-wife team today; too many of these teams come to grief, and in unexpected ways.

Let us assume harmony within the partnership. There is still the market to face, individual editors to cope with, and usually there will be an agent. What if one member of the team has a personality clash with one of these? They say that opposites attract and that there is a positive and a negative pole in every partnership, just as in every storage battery. This is likely to mean that if one member of the partnership gets along fine with a particular editor or agent, the other very likely will not.

Consider the situation from the other end. The editor or agent may find it hard to get along with one or the other member of the team. This can cause the kind of tension that will result in the scuttling of the account. "The letters I get from X," an editor once told me, "are warm and friendly and X can take criticism. But that partner, Y, is a sonofabitch. I am not going to put up with him. You'll have to take the account to another publisher."

If opposites attract, and I believe it to be true, how does an editor or an agent send a single letter to two writers that both recipients are going to like? In the days when I was foolish enough to become involved with collaborations I had to walk a chalk line between the two members of a team in order not to turn one or the other off!

Writing teams are not the only collaborations that fall apart. Look what happens in show business. It seems almost inevitable for two or more humans working together to dissolve their association once big money has given them something tangible to fight over. When individual egos start making waves, one comes to realize how tenuous are business friendships and working alliances.

Bear in mind, too, the possibility that death may interrupt a harmonious relationship between two writers. The surviving member, having functioned for years as half a writer, finds it almost impossible to carry on.

You may decide you are too weak to stand on your own feet, and you may know somebody who seems to be loaded with talent and whom you would like to work with as a partner. So you sell a few books together and then one unhappy day you are told you are no longer needed. The partner has decided to go it alone. You are now in the same critical position as the writer whose partner has died.

There is such a thing as talent drying up. This frequently happens to women during menopause or men in middle age. Personal tragedy can also render a writer incapable of creative thinking. Also, psychoanalysis or a nervous breakdown can have disastrous results. A team of writers is much like a two-engine plane. So long as both engines are functioning the plane stays up in the air. If something happens to one of the engines the plane usually crashes.

Today when two writers appear in my office with only one manuscript between them, I tell them to go away. I would like to tell them to break it up. But, of course, that is none of my business.

9

Stay Away from Grapevines

I SUPPOSE IT IS ONLY NATURAL, IF YOU LIVE IN AN AREA FAR RE-
moved from the publishing center, to seek contact with other
writers in order to compare notes on editors, publishers, agents,
and each other. There are writers' clubs and writers' conferences
scattered all over the country which facilitate this endeavor. There
are groups such as the Mystery Writers of America, the Western
Writers of America, the Authors' Guild, The Dramatists' Guild,
and smaller organizations which periodically bring writers
together. But there is also something sinister known as the
"grapevine," and this I would advise you to stay away from.

Writers are inclined to correspond with other writers who turn
out the same kind of product. Since vast geographical distances
may lie between them, the United States mail proves useful. All
their frustrations, grievances, and antagonisms can be bruited
about in letters—which serve as a kind of cathartic that eliminates
hang-ups and proves as useful as a church confessional. They can
also prove dangerous, especially to one who is naïve enough to
believe what is contained in them.

The fact that one writer gets a larger advance from a publisher
than another is no reason for turning against the editor or the
agent who negotiates for the smaller figure. The business of com-
paring notes on contracts can be unfair and disconcerting. Never
overlook the tendency among writers to boast of their earnings—
much as publishers like to boast, and even lie, about print orders.

31

You can never be sure what to believe as fact and what to dismiss as fantasy.

Gossip constitutes a large part of the written communications that pass among writers. Especially tasty morsels are those bits of gossip having to do with the private lives of men and women in the business.

The best grapevine tender I ever knew was the late Jack Woodford, a compulsive letter writer who maintained a vast circle of pen pals up to the time of his death. He had a penchant for embroidering stories and disseminating them as fact. These often proved most upsetting to their recipients.

Some years ago a group of western novel writers had a grapevine of the sort you might expect to find among a bevy of old crones. An editor seen imbibing several cocktails at lunch was at once set down as an alcoholic. I know one literary agent whose business was almost destroyed by the rumor that he had become a lush. Publishers were accused of tinkering with their royalty statements if they showed too many goose eggs, and if the statements were late they were suspected of impending bankruptcy.

If you must be part of a grapevine, be careful what you have to say. Take it for granted that any information you provide will be distorted as it is passed around. Be no more casual about circulating rumors than you would be about removing your clothes in public.

Writers can be insanely jealous and envious of each other. Do not expect to be sincerely congratulated upon receiving a huge advance or making a movie sale. Chances are your literary pen pals will secretly hate your guts. It was Lucretius who wrote: "How sweet it is to behold from shore another's shipwreck." If you really want to be popular with others on a grapevine, tell only of the disasters that befall you in your pursuit of a literary career.

10

When to Use a Pen Name?

THERE IS AN OLD SAYING IN SPORTS ARENAS: YOU CANNOT TELL the players without a scorecard. In publishing these days you cannot even tell them *with* a scorecard, for half the commercial writers in America are using pen names.

There are many reasons for this. Commercial writers with fantasies about some day becoming literary mammoths prefer to withhold their real names in the belief that to do otherwise might hurt their chances. This is not necessarily true. Even a good writer is entitled to serve an apprenticeship and not be expected to start at the top. J. P. Marquand had no problem switching, under his own name, from his Mr. Moto stories in the *Saturday Evening Post* to a literary career under the Little, Brown imprint, and one could point to many others. Of course, if a talented writer were to start out writing porn, a pseudonym would be imperative.

A more valid reason for using a pen name is that publishers like to corral a name and keep it in the firm. A writer who turns out more than one book a year is usually obliged to use two or more publishers, each of whom may wish to have exclusive use of a particular name and type of writing. This makes it very confusing for the reader who may be interested in identifying the author. One very prolific client of mine uses eight pen names. Since a publisher will demand an option on a particular name, a reader may buy half a dozen books that appear to have been written by different authors when, in fact, all have been written by the same person.

There may be ethnic reasons for using a pen name, but I refuse to buy them. I know of no publisher anywhere who would turn down a property for reasons of personal prejudice against any racial minority

A much more valid reason for using a pen name is the need to conceal your sex identity. At this writing, female viewpoint romances and historical novels are much in demand. A number of these are written by men under women's names. Today it is the male writer who may have reason to disguise his sex in the interest of wider acceptance. The problem George Sand had to contend with in her day no longer exists.

There is still another reason for a name change, one that is purely aesthetic. Some writers do not care for their own names, and their only opportunity to do something about it comes when they publish a book. Publishers also suggest pen names for books in certain categories. (Gothics, for example, often bear pen names that have an eerie ring to them.)

Literary history turns up many famous pseudonyms. Who would not rather read a book by Mark Twain than one by Samuel Clemens? Anatol France is more interesting as a name than Jacques Thibault. Voltaire looks better on a book than François Marie Arouet.

When using a pen name you must decide how you want to have the copyright handled. If you want to conceal your true identity from the reader, you will want it taken out in the publisher's name or in the pen name.

11

Pornography
and Four-Letter Words

EVERYBODY SEEMS TO MAKE MONEY OUT OF SEX EXCEPT THE ACtual purveyors: the prostitutes who are exploited by their pimps, the skinflick performers who are exploited by their producers, and the writers who are exploited by their publishers.

Several years ago I visited a friend who had left New York and gone to the West Coast to become editor for what was, at the time, the leading pornographic publisher in the country. He worked out of a plush office in a handsome building which housed the staff and the presses. Outside I saw the publisher's new Cadillac in the parking lot beside a rather beaten-up jalopy that I knew belonged to the editor. The latter's job was to hire writers to turn out novels calculated to turn readers on. The books were bought outright for modest fees and written under sexy-sounding pen names. It was big business.

More recently the situation for pornographic book publishers has deteriorated. Skinflicks alone may not explain it. There is also reader boredom to be considered. Sodomy, fellatio—all the variations of the sex scene—have been thoroughly explored. These books have lost their shock value and have become corny. Then, too, most of the books put out today by prestigious New York houses not only contain graphic love scenes but also story content as well. Readers are getting more for their money.

Most writers of pornography are either youngsters hoping eventually to make their way up the ladder or they are old-timers on the way down and desperately trying to hang on. Porn editors treat them with mild contempt, much the way pimps treat their hustlers. To all creative talent I would like to say, *Don't get involved.* But I recognize the demands of the stomach and the need for three meals a day.

There was once a fine training school for writers known as "the pulps." These were stories and novels printed on pulpwood paper, and they contained fiction that fell into much the same categories we have today: westerns, mysteries, science fiction, science fantasy, and romance. These pulp magazines were put out by large chain publishers: Hillman, Goodman, Standard, Popular, and many others. Among the editors were many distinguished names: Leo Margolies, Malcolm Reis, Orlin Tremaine, Mike Tilden, Harry Maule, Captain Shaw, Kenneth White, and Donald Kenicott, to name a few. They taught young writers how to plot, how to tag characters, how to handle flashbacks, and how to break a story into beginning, middle, and end. Half the successful writers in America came up via the pulp route; and when the pulps were killed by the paperback books, these same writers were trained and ready for the new market.

Today the closest thing to a beginners' school, though I hate to admit it, is pornography. It produces writers who are poorly trained and ill-prepared for better outlets. As in Sweden and Denmark, pornographic fiction in America has unfirm roots and may eventually disappear. One New York–based firm that used to print 100,000 copies of its editions now prints only 10,000 and admits having doubts about the future.

Of course there has always been pornography in one form or another, but there have not always been pornographic books. Mike Grady, writing in *Newsweek,* supports the belief that in a very few years these books will disappear. Others have predicted they will be absorbed into the output of reputable publishers who no longer shy away from graphically described love scenes.

Legal barriers may some day be erected against pornographic books, but to date such barriers have been made of *papier mâché.* Over the years suits brought by the government have been singularly unsuccessful; *Fanny Hill, Ulysses, God's Little Acre, Tropic of Cancer* are now classics that can be found in any well-stocked bookstore.

Not long ago a Presidential Commission on Sex arrived at this conclusion: "No evidence that exposure to explicitly sexual material plays a significant role in the causation of delinquent or criminal behavior among youths or adults."

You may take it from here. . . .

Then there is the business of four-letter words. We can all look back to our childhoods and remember the titillating effect of certain four-letter words scribbled on a wall and our disappointment at not finding them in the family dictionary. There was a time in my early teens when the sight of a certain four-letter word was enough to turn me on.

In the years following World War II four-letter words appeared with increasing frequency in American novels, and I have always suspected that they had some bearing upon the success of some of the books, especially the war novels, that came out after the shooting stopped. One writer whom I have always considered to be vastly overrated, and to have gained no small measure of his popularity as a result of having been banned in Boston, is Henry Miller. Sly rascal that he was in his prime, he knew the shock value of certain words and lost no opportunity to slip them into his prose.

Today the once taboo four-letter words appear with great frequency, not only in novels but in plays and motion pictures as well. Erica Jong's endless repetition of four-letter words in *Fear of Flying* seems purposely designed to titillate the reader.

What concerns me a little is the likelihood that, through excessive use, four-letter words will eventually produce apathy in the reader or the theatre audience. In some recent movies the script writers seem to throw in as many of them as possible whenever the opportunity arises. The resultant sophomoric effect does nothing to enhance the prestige of the director or the producer.

Used with discretion, four-letter words can still achieve the desired effect, but not all writers are discreet. When Julie Christie turns to her male table companion in a movie called *Shampoo* and bluntly tells him she would like to perform fellatio, the effect is brilliant. Had she used obscene language repeatedly through the earlier scenes the effect would have been negligible.

Not long ago I read the memoirs of one of my favorite editors. He is a gentleman of considerable charm and good taste. In all the years I have known him I have never heard him utter a four-letter word. Yet the title of one of his chapters was "The Publisher as a Shit." Now while there can be no disagreement about the person he was describing, I must confess I found the heading distasteful

37

and most unsuitable as part of a chapter heading in a book of memoirs.

Both in conversation and in print there is a time and a place for four-letter words. But you have to be careful they do not boomerang. I personally like to regard them as ammunition that can be effective only if used sparingly for emphasis on appropriate occasions. As these words become hackneyed from overuse, I sometimes wish we could go back to Chaucer or Shakespeare and recapture some of the fine old Anglo-Saxon obscenities.

I am sure it is respect for good taste and not prudishness or fear of negative reaction on the part of subscribers that restrains such reputable publications as *Time, Newsweek, Reader's Digest,* and the like from using four-letter words in their copy. Seldom are they employable as adequate substitutes for the *mot juste*. Think about this before you sprinkle these little words too freely through your writing. They often define nothing so much as the impoverished mind of the user.

12

What Price Vanity

A VANITY PUBLISHER WILL PRINT ALMOST ANYTHING YOU WANT TO put on paper and for a price. The come-on advertisements that appear in newspapers and magazines offer false hopes to writers naïve enough to believe a publisher has to go out looking for material. The deceptive literature sent out in response to these advertisements has always impressed me as being tasteless and offensive.

It is true that an occasional subsidized book will enjoy a modest sale, either because the writer has produced a work that might have been sold to a legitimate royalty publisher had it been given a harder push or because the writer has a large personal following that can be reached through the mails. But most of the books put out by vanity houses are still-born babies.

The flattering acceptance letters sent out once a manuscript has been submitted would be amusing were it not for the fact that many of the recipients have been known to mortgage their homes or cash in their insurance policies in order to come up with the subsidy money such firms require. I have yet to see a letter from an editor of one of these outfits that has said, "Don't expect to get your investment back because it isn't likely to happen."

Pick up a newspaper anywhere in the country and you will probably find a small advertisement that reads, AUTHORS WANTED. What magic words these are to a disappointed and disgruntled would-be author who sits forlornly beside a pile of rejection slips!

Usually the cost figures, which can range from $3,000 to as much as $15,000, include enough gravy for the publisher to satisfy his appetite even if he fails to sell a single copy. Cost will usually include the binding of a few thousand copies, even though the vanity house knows that an actual binding of 500 sheets will prove more than adequate. The resulting product may look quite professional, but usually it has no place to go except on the author's shelf.

I am often shown books put out by vanity publishers. Both books and the covering letters go immediately into the trash.

Is there nothing then, you may ask, that can be legitimately handled on a subsidized basis? Yes, I think a volume of poetry must of necessity have to be paid for by the author unless it be a collection of poems that have already appeared individually in magazines. Also, a large industry that is planning a giveaway campaign, and is not thinking in terms of possible sales, may want to subsidize a book, perhaps after being rebuffed by the royalty houses. Again, a successful lecturer may find it makes sense to put out books for a captive market.

Books which should *never* be subsidized, in my opinion, are works of fiction, which even the best trade publishers nowadays have a hard time selling; books on philosophical, sociological, religious, and other specialized subjects where lay opinions and theories are worthless; personal memoirs that nobody outside the writer's family is going to pay a dime to read and that might better be typed, Xeroxed, and set aside for the day they can be forced on the grandchildren.

Before considering a vanity deal you should first check on the solvency of the firm selected, which you can do by demanding a bank reference. Samples of the publisher's product should be inspected to be sure he knows how to turn out a professional job and does not put out books with dirty press work, cheap paper, or crude binding. Payment should be made in installments, with enough money held off until publication to make certain the firm cannot profit until delivery of bound copies has been made.

What a lot of writers do not know is that many so-called name publishers—hard and softcover alike—now deal in subsidized books. In a recent political campaign I was asked to find a publisher for one of the Presidential candidates. Much to my surprise I found several good firms had set up special departments to handle this type of business. Quotations I received in this instance included the usual gravy for the house with no promises made regarding use of the firm's regular imprint. One large paperback house has a special imprint for subsidized projects.

My guess is that vanity publishing, a multimillion-dollar business already, is on the rise. There are now publishers in New York that specialize in so-called premium business and approach large industries for possible subsidized deals. There are firms that study each season's crop of nonfiction hoping to find books in specialized areas that might appeal to corporations for use as giveaways. A hamburger cookbook, for example, might appeal to a meat wholesaler; a book on how to ski to a sporting goods manufacturer, and so on.

As legitimate firms get more involved in subsidized publishing, so-called vanity houses may find it difficult to survive. This will call for even greater caution on the part of persons of modest means who may be tempted to pay for publication. There will be hollow promises of bigger and bigger "profits." (The FTC, incidentally, has restrained these firms from using the term "royalty" without qualifying it to mean the percentage of return granted to the author on the *latter's* investment. Normally royalties are the percentage of earnings paid to the writer on sales resulting from the *publisher's* investment.)

Some observers seem to feel that lately there has been an effort on the part of a few of the older vanity publishers to tone down their come-on promotion and stop promising the sky. "A lot of people still get taken in, but many of the vanity firms have improved tremendously," says Carol Nomeyer of the Association of American Publishers. Whether this has been voluntary or the result of FTC coaxing it would be difficult to say. Certainly one may expect vanity houses to continue to respond to FTC coaxing as an increasing number of prestige houses compete for subsidized deals.

Over a thousand books a year are put out at the authors' expense, many of these being the work of college professors who must, as the saying goes, publish or perish. (The unfortunate victims in such transactions are the students who must buy the professors' books when they sign up for a course.) Here again vanity firms must compete with established publishers—theuniversitypresses—who may or may not require their authors to pay.

In the entire range of vanity publishing I can think of only two outstanding successes: *Jehovah's Witnesses*, published by Vantage Press, became a national best-seller because the sect declared it recommended reading for its followers; and *My Years with General Motors*, written by no less a tycoon than Alfred P. Sloan, Jr., and published by McGraw-Hill, found a large readership among those who favor business books.

Librarians as well as reviewers and booksellers shy away from subsidized books because of the limited demand. So numerous are the legitimate new books that even titles put out on a royalty basis are uncertain of places on library shelves. It is highly doubtful that those involved in the dissemination of books will ever overcome their deep-seated aversion to subsidized publishing.

13

The New Copyright Law

AFTER MORE THAN TWENTY YEARS OF DICKERING OVER THE PROBLEM, Congress finally agreed upon legislation for a new copyright law. It was the first complete revision of the law since 1909, and the action was long overdue. It is important for you to know that unpublished as well as published works are covered by the new law and that the term of copyright begins at the time of the work's creation rather than at the time of its publication.

In the past, a literary work was copyrighted either in the name of the publisher or the name of the author for a period of 28 years. Application for renewal could be made in the final year, and an extension could be granted for an additional 28-year period. The new law substantially alters the copyright period. It extends the duration from a maximum of 56 years to the life of the author plus 50 years. It is this alteration primarily that you will want to bear in mind.

Finally, the new law provides that you may reclaim your copyright after 35 years. In the past, publishers have found it possible to hang on to a copyright for the duration of the protection period. This effectively lops off 21 years from the publisher's hold on a property.

There are other interesting changes. After July 1982 it will no longer be necessary for a work to be printed in the United States in order for it to receive copyright protection. Terms of copyright will run through the end of the calendar year in which they would otherwise expire and not just to the particular month in that year that corresponds to the month in which the copyright was taken out. Copyrights now in effect must still be renewed, but the renewal will be for 47 rather than 28 years; those already in their renewal period will automatically be extended to run a total of 75 years from the date of their original publication. The new life-plus-50-year term brings the United States law into conformity with the Bern Convention, which has always had this provision.

Heretofore unpublished works were protected only by common law. I used to be amused by alleged copyright notices on original material submitted to the agency, for I knew such notices were falsified. The new law makes the copyrighting of unpublished works not only possible, but it makes it possible from the date of completion. In other words, it brings them under the protection of statutory copyright, meaning that the federal law henceforth supersedes both common and state law.

The new law makes deposit of the work with the Library of Congress mandatory if it is to receive protection, but it does not require registration. In other words, you do not lose your copyright if you fail to register at the Copyright Office in Washington.

Registration fees, like all other fees, are subject to change; for latest information on the subject you can contact the Copyright Office. You will find these fees a good investment because (1) infringement suits may not be brought, nor may attorney's fees be awarded by the courts, unless your work is properly registered; (2) unless your work is registered, a copyright assignment cannot be recorded.

It is too early to predict how the new law will work out. The Copyright Office will be deluged with mountains of unpublished material from poetry to monographs, essays, business reports, and even advertising copy. But save your sympathy, it will also be taking in millions of additional dollars in registration fees.

As this is being written, the registration fee has already jumped from $6 to $10. You may bet on its going even higher as an increasing volume of paper pours in. Poets and essayists may submit several works for a single fee, obviating the possibility of their being charged excessively.

Substantial coverage is given to the infringement of copyright in the new law. Statutory damages range from $250 to $10,000, according to the length and importance of the material involved and whether or not infringement is intentional. Personnel changes in publishing houses are so numerous that it is always possible for an innocent mistake to occur, such as publishing a work which is believed to be under contract but for which contracts have not actually been signed. The law also provides penalties for those rascals who fraudulently use a copyright notice in the front of a book or make untrue representations regarding a copyright application (up to $10,000 in fines and up to a year in prison).

It is a good law and both authors and publishers stand to benefit from its provisions. After all, a Congressional struggle that took over 20 years to be resolved ought to produce worthwhile results.

PART TWO

ABOUT AGENTS

Ninety percent of everything that is published
commercially is handled by literary agents.
Whether you do your own selling
or work through a middleman,
you should have some idea of what agenting is all about.

1

Finding the Right Agent

IF YOU ARE SHOPPING FOR AN AGENT IT MIGHT BE SMART TO IN-
quire among the publishers whose product you respect and would
like to emulate. Most publishers have lists of the agents they do
business with, but you will find them reluctant—and for very good
reasons—to recommend a particular firm. A self-addressed
stamped envelope should bring an answer to your query, but you
must bear in mind that failure of an agent's name to appear on a
list does not necessarily mean the agent is not reliable. Few middlemen can maintain working relations with all publishers, and
they will have closer contact with some than with others.

I have spent a lifetime peddling literary properties, and yet
there are a number of fine hardcover houses I have never done
business with. I daresay there are editors in New York and Boston
who do not even know of my existence—just as I may not know
of theirs. Because an editor has never heard of Donald Mac-
Campbell does not mean I am *persona non grata* with that editor's
firm. It may only mean I have never gotten around to taking that
editor to lunch.

The agent who is always in the news with blockbuster deals
may be an unwise choice. Even if you should be accepted as a
client, there is the possibility of your being lost in the crowd. A
new writer is often better off with a younger representative who is
eager for business and willing to make the extra effort required to
develop a promising account. Actually the option to choose be-

tween a long-established agent and one still on the way up does not always exist, for the one with the stable of famous names may not let you get past the receptionist.

The size of an agency is something to be considered when making your bid for acceptance. Whereas the one-man or one-woman operation will be in a position to offer you personal attention, the large departmentalized agency is likely to turn you over to some young apprentice out of Vassar or Harvard who is still learning how to sell and how to judge a property's value.

It cannot be repeated too often that agents exist by selling bad books because there are not enough good ones available. Nowadays when so many projects are sold on an outline basis—at least after the groundbreaker has been disposed of—it takes an experienced hand to know what to send to market. When you read that a best-selling book has a history of ten or more rejections, you can safely assume it has been mishandled somewhere along the line, quite possibly by some young reader in a large agency who has been assigned to the job of placing it.

Then there is the personality problem to be considered. Your agent should send off good vibes. Many relationships are doomed from the start for lack of compatibility. I have learned to sniff out a no-no account after a very few minutes of firsthand contact; when getting acquainted by mail it can take much longer. Call it chemical antipathy if you like, it has to be reckoned with. The stores are full of books by able writers whom I would not want to handle, even if I got the 90 percent and they got the 10 percent. You must try to meet an agent in person before you become involved, so that together you can assess the likelihood of a long-term relationship. It is very much the same as entering a marriage: you do not have to be in love, but you had better be damn good friends.

Most agents are inclined toward a particular level of material, and for this reason too you must be sure that you are approaching the appropriate people. There are a few truly *literary* agents—I said a *few*—and these will turn up their noses at anything they regard as trash. There are a great many *commercial* agents who make a good living handling projects for the masses. Fortunately there are also both literary and commercial writers who fit nicely into agencies that share their own interests. But heaven help the literary writer who signs up with a crassly commercial representative, or vice versa!

Good agents make a point of reading everything they send out to a publisher. However there are several who lean on editors and expect them to do their first reading. There is one in particular who, according to a well-known editor, "sends stuff out by the wheelbarrow." Once an agent gets the reputation of being irresponsible in the way he or she sends out material, then the entire clientele has to suffer. You are not likely to find that agent's name on any publisher's list of favorites.

There exists a kind of unvoiced rivalry between editors and agents, probably because the latter make considerably more money for less sweat. If editors are impressed with the shrewd business "savvy" of the leading agents, they are also inclined to test the smartness of newcomers to the field by offering them minimum terms and seeing if they can get away with it. Recently I was shown a contract by a new agent which contained terms so outlandish I could hardly believe my eyes. The lease was for world rights for the duration of copyright; the advance was half what I normally receive from the same paperback publisher, and it was payable in *four* installments. When I told this agent he was getting a rotten deal, he called the editor at once. "We sent you an unagented writer's contract by mistake," he was told apologetically. "Send it back and we'll replace it." I suspect this editor was simply trying to see if he could get away with putting a new agent and an unagented writer in the same bag!

Good agents, like good marriage partners, are hard to find. If you are rebuffed in your attempt to get taken aboard by the agent of your choice, do not despair, for there is a way to go about it and I will explain. Keep mailing your work directly to the publishers who have welcome mats out and, while it takes a lot longer to manage on your own, eventually you will get an offer. Now go back to the agent who has rebuffed you, and place the deal in this agent's lap. What you are doing is handing out a commission in exchange for the agent's attention, and very likely a place among his or her clientele.

Let us now assume you have landed an agent and your honeymoon begins. The question arises, should the agent be expected to handle everything you write? The answer depends entirely upon the policy of the firm. Some agents will even handle poetry by a writer who can turn out successful fiction or nonfiction books. Others will want no part of what they regard as petty business.

In the days when I had contracts with clients, I always spelled out exactly what I would and would not handle. Short stories, articles, poetry, and essays were excluded from any agreement.

Later, when I discarded contracts and began working on a gentle-men's-agreement basis, I began receiving these unwanted efforts from time to time until I was obliged to set a minimum commission of $250 on anything I sold. Since much of this kind of material does not produce enough revenue to make a $250 commission feasible, writers soon stopped sending it in.

Your major problem will lie with the more ambitious projects that you may be excited about but that leave your agent cold. What then? I have lost valuable accounts by turning down things that have subsequently proved salable when sent directly to publishers. Sometimes I have managed to steer a safe course between Scylla and Charybdis by offering these marginal projects, when I consider it expedient to do so, with apologetic notes to the editors suggesting the kind of rejection letter that will not give offense when passed along but that will, at the same time, support my own conclusions.

The line between *publishable* and *unpublishable* is a hard one to draw. An editor who has a gaping hole in the new seasonal list and who is desperately seeking a way to fill it may take on a property which normally he would never accept. This may turn out to be the very property that an agent wanted no part of and returned to the client with regrets. Some agents solve the dilemma of marginal properties by agreeing to take them on to preserve harmony in the relationship and then stowing them away in the horizontal files. Perhaps at a later date—maybe on the occasion of a big killing—they can quietly return the manuscript without making waves. The horizontal files, of course, become a risky solution if the big killing does not materialize!

Agents do not always lose their disgruntled clients to other agents. In recent years a more serious threat to their biggest accounts has come from lawyers experienced in the ways of publishing. Actually, big-money writers do not have to fall out with their representatives before switching to legal representatives. Their accounts simply become too complicated for agents to handle. But legal minds are expensive, and no way will they work for 10 percent. To be handled by an attorney, a writer should have annual earnings in six figures—in other words, he should have a tax problem large enough to allow a generous bite out of income. I am sure this is something you will not have to think about for a while.

2

The Agent
in Today's Market

PUBLISHING HAS BECOME A VERY COMPLICATED BUSINESS, NOT AT ALL like it used to be. For one thing, there are conglomerates everywhere, making it more and more difficult to know who is running the show. A few years back much was made over the taking over of World and New American Library by the Times-Mirror organization of Los Angeles. More recently other giant conglomerates have moved into the business. Gulf & Western now owns Simon & Schuster and Pocket Books, together with Paramount Pictures. MCA engulfs Universal Pictures and Television as well as Putnam and Berkeley Paperbacks. Warner Communications includes Warner Brothers Pictures and Warner Books—formerly Paperback Library. CBS owns Fawcett and Popular Library. RCA owns Random House, Alfred A. Knopf, and Ballantine Books.

Within the publishing business itself, there have been several acquisitions and mergers. Harper & Row has acquired T. Y. Crowell; Grosset has acquired Ace Books and Award Books. Doubleday has acquired Dell Publishing Company. Pyramid Books went public, back to private again, and was finally acquired by Harcourt Brace Jovanovich. No attempt to present a complete list of the changes effected recently can be complete, since they continue to take place year after year.

Where book scripts were formerly offered to one firm at a time, many major properties are now sold at auction, lifting advances into astronomical figures. For paperback rights, a figure of $2,000,000 is no longer an impossibility. Bantam and Avon, two leading paperback houses, have already exceeded this price.

Hardcover publishers are now at a loss to achieve a respectable profit on hardcover rights alone, and more and more become the satellites of paperback houses. Let a reprinter hit upon a bright new category—as Avon did with the erotic historical—and every hardcover house from Doubleday down becomes interested in originals of the same type, buying them at minimal prices and hoping to auction them in six figures. The rights departments of hardcover publishers are the props which hold them above water.

The gap between literary and commercial becomes wider and wider as profits from the former shrink yearly while income from the latter continues to grow. Literary novels can no longer compete with carefully manufactured products geared to motion picture and television as well as to book production. Movie tie-ins frequently become best-sellers. Stanley Newman, vice president in charge of publishing activities at MCA-Universal, states that "half of the best-sellers in paperback are there because of a film or TV show." This conglomerate developed a special department for the purpose of handling these tie-in deals.

Not long ago a lead article in a publication for writers known as *Coda* presented a dismal picture of the literary novelist in today's world. After quoting John Leonard, chief cultural correspondent of the *New York Times* and himself a novelist, to the effect that there were only about a hundred writers in the country who made a living from their books, it went on to present case histories of serious novelists who earned peanuts and concluded with a warning to all writers not to be deceived by news reports of million-dollar sales. Financial success—yes, even in the flourishing commercial areas—is pretty much of a fluke.

Writers who drool over the occasional blockbuster deal must still content themselves, even when working with competent agents, with advances that usually run between $5,000 and $10,000; advances in excess of $10,000 are still exceptions to the rule. This puts a great strain upon the agent-author relationship. "If some unknown Australian can write a book that a reprinter is willing to pay $1,900,000 to acquire, how come that same reprinter wants to offer me a measly $6,000 for my new book?" It is a familiar question, particularly when paperback books are today being advertised on radio and television regularly and when the authors make themselves available for publicity tours around the country.

One explanation is: most books serve as filler material for publishers primarily concerned with promoting their *leaders*. A publisher pays a small fortune for a leader and then spreads what

53

is left of his budget among the hungry writers of category fiction. Fortunately there is plenty of grist available for the mill, so that if one writer balks at a modest advance there will be another ready to snap it up.

Finding writers is no problem; there are more than enough scattered among a hundred or more agencies in New York. Maintaining capable editorial operations, considering the temptation among editors to jump from house to house, is a more worrisome problem. Hanging on to a good editor is more difficult than keeping a good writer in line, especially among the hardcover firms. One recent development has been to let editors have their own imprints—function as satellite publishers within the framework of the overall operation—thus affording them an opportunity to earn over and above a fixed salary and also to get their names on the bookshelves. Many of the new publishers are really not publishers at all, but divisions within the firms that employ them.

Where, you may ask, does the agent fit into this brave new world of publishing? In this field, too, there have been major changes in recent years. It used to be necessary for a middleman to spend long hours, in and out of the office, reading complete manuscripts, or at least sizeable portions of them, in order to secure contracts for his clients. Nowadays, except in deals involving new writers, many projects are sold on an outline basis Where it used to take an agent a day to read two or three offerings, he can now dispose of ten or twenty in the same amount of time. A complete manuscript, which requires the publisher to take less of a gamble, can usually bring a higher advance. But from an agent's point of view it makes more sense to take a little less front money and make more sales.

You may ask, are books better or worse as a result of being commissioned from outlines? On this, editorial opinion is divided. Richard Snyder of Simon & Schuster complains about having to go along with the current practice, "You can't tell whether the book is going to be quality written or not." Some writers seem to feel that once the publisher is hooked they can breeze through the project. My own feeling is that selling on an outline basis is more likely to produce better results because the writer can work without having to worry about the possibility that the whole effort may prove to be a waste of time.

As it would be unreasonable to restrict a creative writer, outlines of novels may be less detailed than the outlines of nonfiction projects (which in my office we call tables of contents). Nevertheless a novelist should follow whatever rough outline he or she offered, inasmuch as the information contained therein is what the publisher is gambling on. It would be very foolish of a writer to change a story after getting an advance on an outline unless the changes were okayed.

Multiple book contracts are common these days, and an agent may sell an entire series of novels or nonfiction projects for an established client with a good track record before a line has been prepared.

In those rare instances where an outline indicates a sure *leader* for a future list, a publisher will pay accordingly. The novel *Shogun* received a $25,000 advance from Dell Publishing Company because the outline, from which it was sold, indicated a substantial sale—which the published book actually realized. I am sure that writers such as John D. MacDonald, Norman Mailer, Irving Wallace, or Harold Robbins receive enormous advances based on their outlines alone, and with the privilege of writing whatever they please. For a publisher or agent to restrict such a writer might be to lose him.

Auctions, nowadays conducted from outlines as well as from complete manuscripts, often result in highly inflated prices. Several hardcover publishers shy away from auctions by agents yet are involved daily in their own auctioning of reprint rights to paperback houses.

All this may tempt you to wonder about the future of the literary agent in publishing. Actually there is no law that says a smart writer cannot run off copies of his project and submit them simultaneously to a number of rich publishers. There is nothing to prevent a highly successful author from ditching his agent in favor of an experienced lawyer who may be in a better position to cope with the intricacies of today's contracts.

Happily for agents, few writers can afford to be handled by lawyers, and fewer still are good enough at business to conduct their own auctions or to get the kinds of deals that are offered when properties are submitted through agency channels. It is my belief that agents will always be a useful, if not indispensable, part of the publishing picture and that writers will continue to seek their services.

Finally, a word about West Coast agents. They alone are permitted to submit properties—published or unpublished—to the studios. If you have a New York agent, you may rest assured that he or she has a working relationship with somebody on the Coast. If you sell directly to a publisher, then the publisher will have the necessary contact. If you are unpublished, no West Coast agent worth having will touch you!

3

Literary Groceries

THE LATE GASTON GALLIMARD, FRANCE'S FOREMOST PUBLISHER, ONCE said that if he could live a second life he would own a pharmacy or a plumbing business, the revenue from which would permit him to publish what he liked in the format he preferred and outside of any commercial considerations. To finance a good book for discriminating readers, publishers today find it necessary to put out products they are not always proud of: "potboilers" as they are commonly described in the trade.

An agent who specializes in commercial properties, as I do, has to feel at times like the grocer who keeps his fruits and vegetables in separate bins. Commercial categories are the equivalent of these bins. The customer, who happens to be the publisher, orders through a staff of editors the gothics, historicals, mysteries, or whatever else may be desired, much as the housewife in a grocery store orders bananas, cucumbers, or lima beans.

Sometimes these categories of fiction are combined in an attempt to offer the public something different. Just as oranges are combined with tangerines to produce temples, so are nurse novels frequently combined with gothics, romances with novels of suspense, historicals with erotica. However, such combinations are exceptions to the publishing rule which has it that, to achieve best results, you keep the groceries in separate bins. One of the most successful of modern paperback operations, Harlequin Books of Canada, concentrates on romances and at this writing leads all competitors in percentage of sales.

The success of category novels is attested to by the announce-ment catalogs of hardcover publishers. Most of them have a back section devoted to commercial fiction. The entries are broken down into the established categories, and it is the income from reprint rights to these books that helps to keep many firms sol-vent. Also, as a result of the enormous popularity of these cate-gory novels, a number of New York agents now specialize in one type or another. Some agencies are rich sources of science fiction; others of westerns or mysteries. My own dispenses the kind of romantic fiction made popular by lending library im-prints; only now, books must be considerably longer owing to the radical increase in the prices of paperbacks. I know of several lady agents who have successfully specialized in material for the women's magazines.

Every time I prepare a batch of published books for my repre-sentatives abroad I find myself trying to make them come out to the nearest pound. If a little under, I add a title; if a little over, I take one off the scale. As in the case of "category bins," on such occasions I cannot help once again applying the analogy of the grocer who dribbles a few extra pods of beans into the bag or puts a few back in the basket.

Over the years I have been contacted by a number of young college girls seeking employment. They all majored in English and clung to the false impression that literature was the name of the game. The discovery that agents send out pounds of mysteries or pounds of romances to foreign markets was usually enough to plunge them into a state of depression.

I believe the most successful writers never set foot inside a college classroom. What the professors of writing usually fail to make clear is the obligation of the seller (in other words, the writer) to become acquainted with the needs of the buyer (who is the publisher). If writers would take the trouble to study the book racks and determine what is currently in demand, slush piles would be much smaller and fewer firms would have to close their doors to direct submissions. I have always advised commercial writers to familiarize themselves with the kind of "grocery" they aspire to produce and to note every aspect of the packaging: the jacket, the blurb, the length, even the retail price—so often deter-mined by the number of pages.

Once upon a time, back in the fifties, mass-market paperbacks sold for 25¢ and ran 50,000 to 60,000 words. Nowadays they may sell for over $2, depending upon the reputation of the author, the size of the book, and the nature of the material.

It seems only yesterday that my agency was peddling hundreds of reprint rights for two lending library publishers whose novels ran around 50,000 words. When the minimum price became $1.25, the short reprint was finished. Writers accustomed to turning out these 50,000-worders were obliged to forget about paperback editions.

Unfortunately, length is not the only problem facing today's commercial writers. The categories themselves rise and fall in popularity, like stock market entries. What happened to Penn Central securities can happen suddenly to the nurse book, the gothic, the sweet romance—in fact, any of the established categories. Bookstore shelves and paperback racks do not always give writers a sure indication of current trends. Nurse books, for example, were still very much in evidence months after publishers had given up putting them out.

The publishing business is in a constant state of flux; it simply refuses to stand still. A writer can turn out dozens of books in the same category and coast along comfortably for years. Then ... boom! The market is no longer there. Today's "groceries" can be tomorrow's unwanted garbage.

4

Reading Fees

I HAVE ALWAYS BEEN OF THE OPINION THAT THE FUNCTION OF AN agent is to *produce* money for writers rather than to relieve them of it. For many years agents who advertise have made a living from reading fees. *Writer's Digest* has been their chief means of reaching the eager yearner who is prepared to do almost anything to get into print. More recently there seems to have been a change in the approach. The spiders are finding new ways to lure innocent flies into their webs. The ads no longer spell out the various charges for looking over a manuscript. However, if reading fees are dispensed with, you may rest assured there will be other unpublicized fees: for criticism, revising, editing, retyping, and so on. On this same subject, I would like to deplore the ambivalent position of writers' magazines that accept money from these agents who advertise and at the same time run articles in which they discourage their readers from paying reading fees. Such hypocrisy is indefensible.

All agents, whether they will admit it or not, are constantly on the watch for talent. Only the stuffed shirts will deny it. So if a new writer sends in a script with a stamped, self-addressed envelope, what does it cost to have a look? Mind you, I said *have a look.* In my office we can frequently dispose of unsolicited material in a matter of minutes. Often a page or two will suffice. If an offering holds attention for a chapter, for half a book, or for the entire manuscript, then obviously it must have merit and be potentially salable. Why then should one pay to have it read?

I think it fair to say that if you send out an unsolicited manu-script and want your book read *in its entirety,* and if you expect criticism, you should be prepared to pay a fee for such service. But I do not believe it should be called a *reading fee. Appraisal fee* would be more appropriate. Often I will refer such a writer to someone whose critical eye I respect, and I do not think $100 is too much to charge for a day of that person's life. (One estab-lished New York agent asks $150 for this kind of inspection, but too often the reading is turned over to inexperienced hirelings.)

If you do not expect criticism, you would be wise to outline your project in a letter of inquiry and to enclose a self-addressed, stamped envelope for reply. An agent is often intrigued by such a letter, especially if it is intelligently prepared, and may ask to have a look at a portion, if not all, of the work in question. Conversely, both time and money can be saved if the agent is unimpressed with either the letter or the description of the manuscript and tells you so straight off.

Do not let yourself be discouraged or defeated by the old argu-ment about overhead and the difficulties of selling unknowns; they do not really hold much water. True, a hardcover publisher thinks twice before taking on an unfamiliar name, but New York has several paperback houses that could not care less about names so long as a book looks salable.

There are still publishers willing to consider the unsolicited manuscripts of unknowns, but their number is thinning out. Slush piles are an expensive part of the editorial operation, for if a firm finds two or three gems in the course of a year it is fortunate. You would be well advised to query a publisher, just as you would query an agent, before sending in a manuscript, just to be sure there is a welcome mat at the door. Certainly an attempt or two at selling this way makes more sense than throwing yourself into the hands of an advertiser who may only be interested in fees.

I am sure not all agents who advertise are bad. But just out of curiosity I sent in a short story to one of them who specifically stated "no reading fees" just to see what would happen. I made it as imbecilic as possible, with plenty of dangling participles and oodles of clichés. A few days later I received a glowing report on the story. I was told I had considerable talent and was destined to succeed, but I was going to need some criticism for a while and this would cost me. After the first few sales, all fees would be dropped. (A safe offer, since my script was almost unreadable.)

My work was meanwhile "certain to be picked up by somebody"—no mention being made of the trash man.

I used to get a kick out of the ads in *Writer's Digest,* which these days are considerably toned down. Printing publishers' checks was a favorite gimmick that worked for years, the checks being laid out in such a way as to make the publisher's name and the amount paid plainly visible while leaving undecipherable the dates, the names of the authors, and the titles. Fortunately, fee-snatching is no longer the thriving business it used to be. Writers today are either poorer or more sophisticated.

5

Thieving Agents

THE LONDON AGENT, DAVID HIGHAM, ONCE TOLD HOW, UPON arriving in New York many years ago, he was immediately swept off to a "coming-out" party. He was at a loss to know what to say to the guest of honor, and no wonder. The party was being given for a literary agent just released from Sing Sing prison where he had served time for ripping off his clients. Though detestable, the practice is not uncommon. The great Somerset Maugham once allegedly defended an agent suspected of ripping him off by saying the man was so charming he could not bring himself to prosecute.

In the publishing business, as I explained earlier, anything interesting that happens—and scandalous doings are always interesting—gets bruited about over luncheon and cocktails. It would appear to be impossible to circulate among editors and publishers and not get to know who the dishonest agents are. Yet, in spite of their flourishing grapevines, writers seldom find out before they have tumbled into their greedy clutches.

The thievery does not usually start with the signing of the contract, for advances are spelled out clearly and not many agents choose this time for shenanigans. More commonly they will "forget" to pay off when the semiannual accounting is made.

Let me illustrate how it usually works. Client X signs a contract and pays the agent 10 percent of the advance—although there is one agent in New York who charges 15 percent. Then silence. No more money appears to have come in. So the client writes to the publisher and complains that his book has earned no royalty. The publisher writes back that, on the contrary, the book has earned a very nice royalty that has been duly turned over to the agent of record in the contract. (Where there is an agency clause in a contract, the agent's receipt of all monies legally discharges the publisher of his financial obligation should that money be filched.) Queried about his failure to pay, the agent pleads guilty to absentmindedness and promptly sends his client a check, unless in the meantime he has left the scene.

From stories I have heard, the second most popular rip-off involves revenue from foreign sales. Before you give an agent power of attorney, you had better be 100 percent sure of his integrity. But even without power of attorney, there is nothing to prevent an unscrupulous agent from making sales abroad and keeping your money. Magazine sales are usually consummated without formal contract, and here the pilfering is easy. Book publishers are more careful to make certain that contracts are legally signed and witnessed.

One of the country's leading mystery writers, whose name I will protect since the story does little credit to his intelligence, once related how a lady agent kept pleading guilty to her inability to get him foreign sales. His friends in the mystery field all did well in such countries as Italy, France, Germany, and Scandinavia—where whodunits have always been popular. But somehow she did not have any luck, even though she worked with one of the biggest agencies in London that handles foreign rights all over the Continent. Exasperated by his agent's failure to sell translation rights, he wrote to London and asked how come. To his horror he received a letter informing him that several thousand dollars in foreign revenue had been sent to his representative in New York, and with the letter came a detailed accounting of the sales. When confronted with irrefutable evidence, the agent confessed to having kept the money. In time she paid off what she had stolen and apologized.

Recently I received a letter from a writer who had been working with a lady agent for nine years before she discovered she too was being robbed of her foreign earnings. She asked me if I would take her on. "The Scots have a good reputation for honesty," she wrote. "I only hope that your name is really MacCampbell."

Another successful mystery writer once invited me to his downtown apartment with a view to leaving his agent and joining me. I asked him what had happened. He explained that he had put together an anthology of short stories and collected a certain fee. Upon checking with the publisher, this writer was surprised to learn that the amount actually paid was twice what the agent had represented. When he asked his agent for an explanation, he was told that the other half was a fee for putting the anthology together.

I am sure that the files of the Better Business Bureau—to say nothing of the Authors' Guild—are crammed with similar stories involving dishonest agents. Yet a writer has no sure defense. Some publishers will continue to buy books from agents they know to be thieves because they can make money by doing so, and, after all, they are not the writer's keeper. But let the publisher himself be victimized and it is a different story.

I once had lunch with a literary agent notorious for his wheeling and dealing. I wanted to pick his brain. To my surprise he told me he had a dummy publishing house for which he bought books personally and then, representing the dummy publisher, resold them for a substantial profit. (This is the same agent who boasts of soaking writers for 15 percent commissions.)

Even an honest agent must sometimes have to cope with temptation, especially when dealing with Hollywood. Many West Coast middlemen have amassed fortunes by buying rights cheap, usually through an intermediary, and reselling for enormous profits. New York agents are rarely involved in such practices for, while they might very well pick up a hot property cheaply, they would not likely have the outlet for resale.

New York agents, however, face temptation in a somewhat different way. I have had more than one independent producer approach me, after setting a movie deal with my office, with a proposal to sign false contracts. Having made a legitimate deal with the author for a modest sum of money, he must now put his package together and go to the bank for backing. With forged papers he could show the bank that he had shelled out several times the amount actually paid for the property. (Of course if I went along I would be "taken care of.")

In television much the same shenanigans take place. I once represented a mystery writer who worked for a New York producer. He did very well for as long as the series stayed on the tube and once, over a few too many drinks, he told me why. "Every time I write a teleplay I have to let the producer have a bite of my fee." Me, I do not get involved with television. But had I represented my client in this kind of transaction I would probably have been offered a bite of the producer's bite to keep my mouth shut. I often wonder how much of the trash a TV viewer is subjected to gets produced on some basis other than merit.

Why do some agents steal? I suspect because they are hungry. To live on 10 percent is not easy, and the smart agent who wishes to preserve his reputation for honest dealing is entitled to have some kind of aboveboard gimmick working for him. One New York agent I know has been successful in packaging deals for paperback houses. He hires writers for series ideas of his own devising and pays them out of the gross received from the publisher. Another agent creates book ideas and doles them out for 5 percent over standard commission; I see nothing wrong in this, although I have never thought of charging a writer for such services.

The agent who simply wraps up manuscripts and sends them out can hardly be expected to thrive. A major operation, alimony payments, a stack of unpaid bills may tempt such an agent to break the Eighth Commandment. But opportunities for theft are much greater in almost any other business than publishing. Why then pick on the poor writer who usually makes 90 percent of what may be described as "peanuts"?

Dear Agent:
Comments
on Letters of Inquiry

IN EACH DAY'S MAIL THE ESTABLISHED AGENT RECEIVES A NUM-
ber of inquiries from writers in search of representation. These
come, in my case, from people who have read my books in their
local library, found my name on some publisher's list of recommended agents, or been recommended by some client who, often
for solid reasons, has asked to remain nameless.

With so many publishers refusing to consider material sent in
directly, the number of these inquiries increases to the point
where only the ones with return postage are likely to be answered. To give you an idea of the typical approach, I have singled out a few of the letters, boiling down the gist of their contents
and appending a thought or two about each:

> Dear Mr. MacCampbell:
> I am twenty-two years of age and have just completed my
> first novel. It runs 80,000 words and deals with the subject of
> adultery. Some of my friends have read it and think it's
> great.
>
> Sincerely,

Comment: A twenty-two-year-old writer on this subject is in water
over his head. As a matter of fact, a twenty-two-year-old writer is
too young to write a novel about anything.

Dear Mr. MacCampbell:
I picked your name out of the Yellow Pages because it is Scottish and I am Scottish too. I am a fifth-grade teacher of English and I have written three novels, all unpublished. I need somebody to handle them for me on a commission basis.

Sincerely,

Comment: The very worst way to pick an agent is by the sound of a monicker. This writer is obviously not very bright. She did not even bother to tell me what her novels were about!

Dear Mr. MacCampbell:
I am sending you a Xeroxed copy of my 40,000-word love story. It is my first effort and my husband thinks it is very good. Please let me know frankly what *you* think of it.

Sincerely,

Comment: A husband is the worst possible judge of a wife's writing ability. Also, if the writer were on her toes and familiar with the market, she would know that 40,000 words do not a novel make. She enclosed a stamped envelope, so I wrote back and told her to forget it.

Dear Mr. MacCampbell:
I have written a book of 100,000 words. It is a war novel. I am sending each of fifty agents six pages of the book to read. Then on the basis of their response I will decide which one to work with.

Sincerely,

Comment: Not all lunatics are in asylums.

Dear Mr. MacCampbell:
I am a divorcee, thirty-two years old and a former beauty queen. I have written a very sexy autobiographical novel about my life with four former husbands. Do you think you could find time to read it? It runs 90,000 words and since I have no typewriter I have written it out in longhand.

Sincerely,

Comment: She enclosed return postage. I told her nobody, but nobody, would read her book in longhand, but that next time she was in town any male agent would be happy to take her to lunch.

Dear Mr. MacCampbell:
I have sold three novels through three different agents. (He mentions their names, all well-established middlemen.) I now have my fourth novel in shape and ready to send out. Would you be interested in seeing it?

Sincerely,

Comment: An agency-hopper, obviously! Both letter and stamped self-addressed envelope went into the trash.

Dear Mr. MacCampbell:
You may remember me. Back in 1958 you came to see me about being my agent. I wasn't at home and you left a card with my wife. If you are still interested let me know.

Sincerely,

Comment: This one returned my call twenty years too late.

Dear Mr. MacCampbell:
I am a teacher of writing in the local college and I have completed a novel which I think has good movie possibilities. Would you care to see it?

Sincerely,

Comment: Since he enclosed a stamped self-addressed envelope I had to write back and tell him that, from my experience, teachers of writing seldom knew how to write.

Dear Mr. MacCampbell:
I have a nonfiction book on health care which has been turned down by seven publishers. I still think it is a good book and would like you to have a look.

Sincerely,

Comment: It's possible but quite unlikely that seven publishers can be wrong. I passed this one up.

Dear Mr. MacCampbell:
I read your Writing for Publication and think it's the best book on writing ever written. You tell it like it is. I would be proud to have you represent me.

Sincerely,

Comment: The flattery caught my attention, but he failed to mention what he wanted me to represent. So it was wasted.

Dear Mr. MacCampbell:
You may remember me. Ten years ago I sent you my novel entitled *The Lost River.* You gave me some good criticism and I have been working on it ever since. Would you like to take another look?

Sincerely,

Comment: A writer who spends ten years reworking the same book is never going to make an agent any money. He could have turned out five more books in that time, and maybe one or two might have been salable. A one-book writer—unless it be a Margaret Mitchell—no agent needs.

Dear Mr. MacCampbell:
I have a definative book on acupuncture and would apreciate it if you would examine it with a view to representing me. That is if you think the book is saleable.

Sincerely,

Comment: I know, I know. There are some very good writers who can't spell, but at least they make an effort to do so.

Dear Mr. MacCampbell:
I am a retired Colonel in the Air Force and am planning to spend the rest of my life writing fiction. Would you care to handle me?

Sincerely,

Comment: I wished him luck with his hobby.

Dear Mr. MacCampbell:
I have what I think is a pretty good log on the fire. I wonder if you would be interested. It is the story of a young Jewish boy who marries an Irish girl and they adopt an Indian child who has leprosy. The story runs 200,000 words and is written in blank verse.

Sincerely,

Comment: I advised the author to remove the log from the fire and insert the manuscript.

Dear Mr. MacCampbell:
I have written a book on volcanoes which has been enthusiastically acclaimed by readers at Macmillan, Doubleday and Morrow. Would you like to see it with a view to taking me on as a client?

Sincerely,

69

Comment: I strongly advised this writer to go back to those three enthusiastic readers and get one of them to buy him.

Dear Mr. MacCampbell:
I have sold over 50 novels to West Coast publishers. They're all very sexy and deal with sodomy, incest, child-molesting, bestiality and necrophilism. Am I ready for New York publishers?

Sincerely,

Comment: I wrote back and told him he was years ahead of the local publishers who were still preoccupied with rape, homosexuality, and simple fornication. I suggested he try again in five years.

These are a few of the no-nos that turn up among the inquiries. How then should you go about approaching an agent without looking ridiculous?

I am most likely to respond to inquiries from writers between the ages of thirty and fifty who show evidence of having read and studied the kind of material that publishers are currently offering, who have some idea as to acceptable length requirements, and who have not already shopped around and are approaching an agent as a last resort. If you are a nonfiction writer I would like a list of credentials: for example, publishers' names, titles, dates. If you are interested in selling fiction, I would like some indication as to your chosen category, whether it be gothic, mystery, historical, romantic suspense, sweet love, or whatever. Also, as mentioned before, a self-addressed, stamped envelope is most likely to provoke a response.

PART THREE

ABOUT
PUBLISHING

Sections 2 and 3 are for book writers only.
The other sections should be of some interest
to all who are endeavoring to write for money.

1

The Guessing Game

PUBLISHING HAS BECOME, AS *Newsweek* ONCE DESCRIBED IT, "A floating crap game." In his book *The Middle Man*, veteran agent Paul Reynolds summed it up neatly. "Authors," he wrote, "assume that publishers know what will sell and how to conduct their business to obtain the maximum sale. Actually publishers are in the twilight zone of being amateurs."

It takes money to put out books. Roger Straus is an example of a well-financed publisher who ran his business at a loss for years before breaking into the black. Others, starting out with little capital and no back list, have been less fortunate. It is sometimes difficult to put one's finger on the cause of failure, since the merger of an unsuccessful firm with a successful one usually blurs the former's mistakes. Business and textbook publishers run less risk in their operations since they usually know what they are doing. Trade book publishers seldom do. Dan Green of Simon & Schuster put it frankly when he said, "We're all wrong most of the time."

Today a hardcover novel often depends on a reprint or a book club sale to lift its publisher out of the red. Since neither of these sales can be assured, it is in this area that the greatest losses occur. To be sure, there are occasional jackpots, but the publisher has to be lucky to hit one. When he does, it is news. You get to read all about it in the news weeklies and the daily press. When Lippincott, for example, bid over $400,000 for an adventure story about survivors of a plane crash in the Chilean Andes and sold reprint rights for around a million dollars before the book was even written, *that* was news.

For the publisher the gamble unfolds in several stages, any of which can prove costly. First there is the acquisition gamble in which the editor has a hand; his judgment is important, but is frequently overruled by the sales department or by the publisher himself. (Few editors have autonomy, although they like to think they do.)

Once a property has been acquired there is the print-order gamble, a significant one thanks to skyrocketing manufacturing costs. The remainder tables in bookstores all over the country bear ample proof of erroneous guesses as to the number of copies of a book the public is prepared to absorb.

Then comes the advertising gamble, actually not so worrisome since appropriations are based on advance orders. A book that dies before its date of publication is not likely to be revived thereafter. But even substantial advance orders can be fraught with danger for publishers who pour a percentage of their anticipated profits into advertising, for it is common knowledge that booksellers order on a protected basis and can return their unsold copies.

What helps to compensate a publisher for all his bad gambles is the book that takes off under its own power, fueled by word-of-mouth advertising that costs not a cent. *Jonathan Livingston Seagull* was a notable example of this kind of phenomenon. Raymond Hagel of Macmillan thought that, with luck, it might sell 10,000 copies; it has sold over 6,000,000 and reprint rights went for $1,100,000. It is jackpots like this that keep the gambling spirit alive. *Jaws* is another example. Bought for a modest advance, it turned into one of Doubleday's all-time best-sellers. And I very much doubt if the one and only novel written by an amateur named Margaret Mitchell and called *Gone With the Wind* was ever supposed to make literary history at Macmillan.

Editors frequently complain that publishers do not allow them enough freedom of selection. However, considering today's costs and the competitiveness of modern publishing, the editor is better off not having to bear on his own shoulders the burden of failure. When a book bombs, there are usually two or more staffers to share the responsibility.

Considering the risks in trade publishing, is it any wonder that most of the big hardcover companies allot a portion of each seasonal list to the safer established categories of fiction? For one thing, a category does not usually expire overnight. Slowly diminishing sales over a period of years give a publisher ample advance warning to duck out. Category books have always been fairly sure bets for the reprint market, and, while they seldom turn into blockbusters, they do provide bread-and-butter income. Doubleday, McGraw-Hill, Morrow, Holt, Rinehart & Winston, Simon & Schuster, Dutton, Dodd, Mead, and others have for many years been able to defray the cost of their overhead with mysteries, westerns, and romances. Other than the categories, it is anybody's guess what makes a trade book sell. Nobody really knows the answer.

Despite the flood of nudie magazines and pornographic movies that have made sexual titillation as common as indigestion, sex is still a magic ingredient in books. You even find it in cookbooks: *Food for Lovers, Cooking With Aphrodesiacs, Sex and the Food You Eat.* Publishers still find it possible to make best-sellers out of books telling the reader how to make love.

The question is no longer "Should there be sex in the book?" but "How can we make the sex respectable?" Women enjoy being turned on by graphic descriptions of lovemaking as much as do men, but they do not like to have their tastes made obvious by lurid titles and sensational cover art. *Fear of Flying* thus becomes an ideal title for a book which, while crammed with four-letter words and sexy doings, can be read unashamedly in public. *Portnoy's Complaint*, a literary treatment of self-abuse, looks innocuous on a bookseller's shelf. Before that, Lolita—which in the hands of a pornographer would have been just another dirty book—enjoyed the same aura of respectability. It was literature—or "lecherature," if you prefer. Sex wrapped in cellophane.

Writers such as Harold Robbins, Irving Wallace, Jacqueline Susann, whom editor William Targ puts in the class of "high schlock," give further dignity to their characters' sexual shenanigans by having their men and women in positions of power and importance. They are never pimps or prostitutes. Nobody is embarrassed to be caught reading these writers in public, which is one reason why they can turn out so many best-sellers.

With the constant exploitation of sex in fiction, it would seem inevitable that sales must gradually decline. In an effort to fortify themselves against such an eventuality, publishers have discovered another magic ingredient: nostalgia. People like to read about sex, but they also like to read about the past. The novel

Ragtime, with virtually no sex, became a top best-seller because it brought back the days of Houdini, J. P. Morgan, and Henry Ford. The magic years of childhood can always be counted on for sales. Salinger discovered a gold mine in vanished youth long before nostalgia became a viable commodity, along with sex, in the bookstores.

You must be ever aware of the fashions in fiction that come and go. Once there was the farm novel, the war novel, the picaresque romance, the business novel. The publisher who adheres to today's fashions minimizes his gamble and maximizes his chances of making a killing through reprint or book club sales. Why, you may ask, is there not more originality in editorial selection when so many far-out books do very well? The answer is simple: it is too risky. Why take unnecessary chances?

In the editorial guessing game the publisher enjoys an advantage over the writer and the agent. By the time a fashion has been established it may already be on the way out. The editor who encourages a particular type of book because currently it happens to be selling, may have to reject it by the time it is drafted. That is why I think it is a mistake to write a complete book on speculation. Best to get your project signed up as quickly as possible on the basis of a good outline and perhaps a few sample chapters, then let the publisher worry about what lies ahead.

Since the selection of salable properties is largely a guessing game, an editor with any degree of sophistication must be willing to laugh off mistakes. The story is told of one Joan Campbell, an editor in a hardcover house, who turned down *Kon-Tiki* with a report to her publisher that read as follows: "Who in hell wants to read about a bunch of crazy Scandinavians floating around the ocean on a raft?" After the book became a top best-seller and remained as such for several weeks, Ms. Campbell dug out her rejection report, framed it, and hung it over her desk. If only there were more editors like that—prepared to teach themselves the importance of humility in judging a property that is different!

Whatever it is that makes a book popular with the public, it is not advertising. Once a book has exhibited certain magic ingredients—sex, violence, nostalgia, or whatever—and once it has gained acceptance through word-of-mouth enthusiasm, paid advertisements can be instrumental in prolonging its active life. But they can never put a book on the best-seller lists, and you had better believe it.

Writers maintain their shabby existence at the discretion of editors who, in many instances, are still learning their craft. A small percentage of them circumvent editorial barriers and back their own efforts financially, often without having to turn to the vultures in the vanity business. They do this because they know that editors can be wrong.

Take the case of a book called *Mandingo* that appeared back in 1957 through the auspices of an obscure firm in Virginia. Kyle Onstott, a sixty-nine-year-old Californian, had a hunch that he had created a readable property. He was not about to accept defeat at the hands of the New York editors who wanted no part of a plantation novel in which the planter's wife bedded down with a black slave whom the planter, after killing his wife, saw fit to boil in a vat of hot water. Everybody laughed at the idea of such a story except the public who bought nearly 3,000,000 copies in hard covers. Fawcett's reprint department subsequently sold another 5,000,000 copies. Result? A whole new category of light fiction was born and Onstott himself made subsequent contributions to it, much to the delight of the suburban housewives who became his fans. Too bad there are not more Kyle Onstotts around today!

2

Why Good Books
Are Rejected

MOST LITERARY SLUSH IS VERY BAD. STILL IT IS ONE OF THE SAD FACTS
of publishing that some unsalable books—both fiction and nonfiction—are actually quite literate and capable of being enjoyed
by the few. For instance, a brilliantly executed treatise on sociology may be turned out by a business executive who lacks the necessary credentials. A compelling study in ethnic relations may be
offered by a professor of mathematics who is unknown outside
his chosen field. A lawyer may have a viable plan for solving the
Middle East problem, but he is not a recognized authority on foreign affairs. It may be a sensitively written novel in blank verse, it
may even be a 200,000-word mystery novel too tightly plotted to
be condensed, or a biography of some little-known character in
history. Odds are that none of these works will ever see the light
of day.

Although in some cases it may be unfortunate, nonetheless it is
a necessary prerequisite that a nonfiction work in a specialized
area must be produced by an authority to be salable. The first
thing an editor asks when told what a project is all about is: Who
wrote it? The label must match the contents. Who would think of
buying a can of soup from the Fuller Brush Company or a suit
tailored by Castro Convertibles? Yet intelligent men and women
labor hard over projects which have no chance of publication on a
royalty basis.

Fiction, as we just discussed in "The Guessing Game," is subject to the rapidly changing interests of the buying public. Many thoroughly readable manuscripts get turned down because they are not salable in the current market. If you try to satisfy editorial requirements by reading the latest published works in a particular category, you must bear in mind that these books may have been acquired a year or two before and that the market for this category may no longer exist.

A recent rejection by a paperback house of an original historical contained this comment, "The 200,000-word length is wonderful, but the story is disappointing." The longer the book nowadays the better its chances, since no distributor has as yet set a ceiling price on paperback fiction. An excellent novella of, say, 40,000 words will find few takers unless the author is a household name like Philip Roth; without his reputation, *The Breast* could never have been published.

Turning back to nonfiction, you ought not to overlook the part that political bias plays in determining what shall and what shall not be published. Authors of so-called right-wing books, regardless of their credentials, have always found it difficult to gain acceptance. At one time I represented a number of United States Senators, and I experienced the futility of trying to promote the ones on the Republican side of the aisle. Many editorial doors are closed to all but the liberal Democrats.

I once secured a contract for a Washington correspondent to write a book about Richard Nixon long before his fall from grace. The author was highly respected in his field, but he had the misfortune, unbeknownst to the editor who signed him up, to be a conservative. His book, when finally delivered, was turned down cold because it was too "soft" on Nixon. The editor who rejected it, a bleeding-heart liberal, undoubtedly took great pleasure in giving my client the shaft. Now can you imagine a book being turned down in this brutal fashion because it was too soft on Jack Kennedy or Lyndon Johnson?

The publishing business is weighted heavily on the liberal side. Let us imagine a book by an anthropologist that attempts through scientific research to establish as fact that the black man's brain is smaller than that of his white brother. Such a thesis would have one devil of a time getting published. Or suppose it were a book in defense of the white minority in Rhodesia: I would hate to have to try and sell it!

Happily sex is no longer a *raison d'être* for turning down a manuscript, fiction or nonfiction. But think back a few years, and consider how many excellent works must have come off the type-writers of talented authors only to be passed up because editors could see no way of sanitizing them for publication. Today the very opposite is true and, amusingly enough, many a novel is rejected because it lacks sufficient sex interest.

What I am trying to say to you is: Not all rejected manuscripts are bad. Just as "many a flower is born to blush unseen and waste its sweetness on the desert air," so many a readable manuscript is destined for the author's attic because, for any of the variety of reasons discussed above, it does not happen to be right for today's market.

3

Publishers' Dirty Tricks

I ONCE ASKED THE AUTHORS' GUILD TO MAKE AVAILABLE TO ME ITS file on dirty publishing practices so that I could present them here. To my astonishment, I was told it would be impossible. Such matters must apparently be kept a deep, dark secret within the membership.

Unfortunately, no author or agent can be conversant with all the trickery that goes on in what was once a gentleman's business. I can reveal here only what I know firsthand, along with such information as I have been able to pick up at the lunch table.

Let me start with the paperback publishers who, while they have done much to keep me solvent, have engaged in practices that should make them hide their heads in shame.

One vicious practice, which deceives readers more than it does authors, is the faking of a copyright. Some firms have used roman numerals so small it would take a magnifying glass to reveal what they are. Many works in public domain are covered by the words "all rights reserved" when no rights are reserved at all. This is much like the vintner who prints on his labels "bottling date reserved."

Then there is the matter of titles. The FTC decrees that if the title is changed, the original must appear on the cover. A cute publisher can resort to almost invisible type. Worse still, he may decide to conceal the original title from the reader. Many of the books I have sold for reprint have undergone title changes two or three times. Yet it is not the agent's place to rat on his customers. There is a legal principle known as *caveat emptor:* let the buyer beware. Can you imagine what would happen to an agent's business if he or she were to lodge a protest against this deception or, worse still, turn in a report to the FTC?

Changing a book's title is permissible if the original appears on the cover, but changing the author's name is something else. Here again an agent has to look the other way. Many times when I receive copies of a paperback reprint I have to get the editor to tell me who wrote it! If both title and author undergo changes, identification is almost impossible. When offering such a camouflaged book abroad, care must be taken to be sure it has not already been sold under other labels.

I once asked a leading paperback publisher why, when he puts out a book for the umpteenth time, the previous printings are not listed in front. Some books go through ten or more printings over a period of years, but you will often find only the original copyright date with no record of the book's later history. The answer is that there happens to be strong wholesaler resistance to books that come out too many times. If the printings are not listed, who is to know?

Another dirty trick perpetrated on an unsuspecting public is the publication of anthologies containing a short piece by some famous author whose name is certain to sell copies. Although the piece may run only two or three pages, this does not prevent a publisher so inclined from spreading the famous name in giant letters across the cover, thus leading the buyer to believe he or she has stumbled upon an unknown work by a favorite author. The FTC has fought against this deception for years, but the practice continues.

Paperback publishers count on a certain degree of naïvete among buyers in the hinterlands. Thus, when they hear of a book that has spawned a forthcoming blockbuster movie under the same title, they will quickly commission a similar project and give it a title close enough to cause confusion but not close enough to invite legal action. A shrewd ex-publisher at New American Library used to boast of such achievements, but pity the poor purchaser who mistakes the counterfeit for the real thing.

Spurious biographies of celebrities have flooded the paperback racks in recent years, but publishers are beginning to wonder if they are worth the tempests they stir up. Not long ago a paperback editor told me of his desire to get an authorized biography of a famous black singer. He went to Motown to seek permission to do the book and was refused.

"So what is to prevent me from having a writer turn out a biography in spite of you?" the editor asked bluntly.

"There is nothing to prevent this," he was told with equal bluntness. "After all, it's a free country. But if you do it, we will sue."

"You wouldn't stand a chance in court," was this editor's reply.

"No, but we could make it uncomfortable for you by taking legal action. Would your publisher want to go through the agony of court proceedings?"

Since publishers have a horror of going to court, this kind of threat can be very dissuasive.

From the book buyer's point of view, an unauthorized biography can be most misleading. That which is accepted as factual material can be no more than a facile romanticization of a subject's career, yet glowing enough in its implications to circumvent any possible charge of libel or invasion of privacy.

Hardcover publishers play dirty tricks of a different kind. Here, unagented writers are always considered fair game for exploitation. The 10 percent that they think they are saving is often offset by up to a 50 percent loss in profit. The Authors' Guild once printed in its bulletin a list of fourteen ways in which a publisher can rip off an author—information made available only to its members.

One firm that I have dealt with has a clause in its contract that permits subsequent printings in quantities of 2,500 copies at the same low 10 percent royalty rate that was paid on the first 5,000. This gimmick could keep a writer forever at the 10 percent level if the publisher wanted to keep putting out printings of 2,500 each, instead of allowing the sliding scale to rise to 15 percent.

Another of their dirty tricks is to hastily produce a book that has been bought for the *first* serialization by a major magazine so that it appears in hardcover before the magazine can run it. This makes the magazine deal a *second* serial sale, which entitles the hardcover publisher to 50 percent of the magazine's payment instead of the 10 percent he would have received had the magazine version appeared first. It can and does happen.

A ruthless publisher can be adamant about a delivery date. Normally, if missed by only a few weeks, and assuming the firm has been notified of the delay, there is no great sweat. Nevertheless, a writer who misses up on the delivery date of a hardcover book runs the risk of having his work unceremoniously dumped if, at some time following the signing of the project, other books on the same subject should happen to turn up in the bookstores. I feel for the publisher whose horse, on such an occasion, is the last one out of the starting gate. But I cannot help believing it is dirty business for him to use a technical escape clause in his contract as an excuse for squirming out of a deal.

You may ask, do publishers deliberately cheat writers? If so, the charge would be difficult to prove. Juggling the figures is most unlikely if the bookkeeper or controller is employed from outside the immediate family. It is more likely to occur if the person who keeps the records happens to be the publisher himself or his wife. It is always possible to "forget" to pay up if the account is un-agented. Mental lapses of this sort, I know for a fact, are not uncommon. And who can safely draw the line between dishonesty and a faulty memory?

Before describing another dirty trick that publishers like to play on the innocent, an explanation is necessary about the way books are sold to the public. There was a time when booksellers had to use extreme caution in their buying or else find themselves soon out of business. Publishers' representatives—the men who carry the season's output around with them and make personal calls on the buyers—used to have to do some pretty fancy talking to get stores to stock the works of little-known authors. That was before books were sold on a protected basis. Today the bookseller takes less of a risk. He is offered merchandise on a protected basis, and unsold copies may be returned, if still in "mint" condition, after interest in the property has waned.

Since the publisher has gone to the extent of gambling his money on a book that may or may not sell, he is interested naturally in not overextending himself when paying out royalties. Advance sales are no sure indication of how a book is going to go, since he can expect what may amount to substantial returns from the booksellers.

To protect himself as best he can against this eventuality, the publisher retains a chunk of the author's royalties come payment time. It is here that the dirty trick comes into play, for it is possible for a disproportionate amount of money to be withheld. Some firms will withhold money long after the unsold copies have been returned—for as long as two or three years. When I have complained about the unfairness of this, I have usually been accommodated with an additional royalty payment and sometimes even an apology.

Foreign publishers are no more ethical than their American

counterparts. Honest agents abroad will tell you without hesitation that there are publishers in their countries whom they cannot deal with in good faith. Their number would seem to increase as one moves south. Warm sunshine seems to encourage chicanery. My worst experiences have usually been in South America and sections of the Middle East, although some years ago I was ripped off good and proper by a slimy gentleman who operated out of Canada—of all places! Scandinavian, British, Dutch, and German publishers are usually honest—I shall not cast aspersions upon the last-named country simply on the basis of one very unfortunate personal experience with a firm no longer in existence which, after paying for material over a period of time, decided it would be cheaper simply to appropriate it, never suspecting it would turn up in a foreign bookstore in New York City!

One of the favorite dirty tricks played by foreign publishers upon American authors is to lease a book for a specified period of time—let us say for five years—with the understanding the rights will revert when it is out-of-print. My former Paris representative, the late Jacques David, once warned me about this possibility. A publisher might set aside X number of copies of his edition so that he could, if necessary, present them in court as evidence of the fact that his edition was still very much in print and that the rights, therefore, need not be reverted under the contract provision governing reversion.

4

Editors on the Move

EDITORS OFTEN MAKE ME THINK OF GIANT GRASSHOPPERS THE WAY they hop from place to place. Fully aware of the fact they are more poorly paid than most garbage collectors, they must be constantly on the watch for some new spot that offers a better deal. It is a common experience for a writer to be taken to lunch by an editor for the purpose of going over a viable project only to have the writer learn a few weeks later that the editor has vanished. *Literary Market Place* is already dated in at least one respect by the time it is off the press. Many of the editors it has positioned with a particular house will have moved elsewhere.

Editors are not to be envied. They sweat and scrounge around for some evidence—usually in the form of a wage increase—that they are ascending the ladder of success, only to find that the upper rungs, when approached, are rickety. While they are looking around for better financial returns, their publishers may be looking for people who can do the same work for less money.

Once upon a time, when editors were less insecure, writers and agents found it possible to call on them during working hours to chat about business. Today such chummy visits are less common, for editors are always in and out of conferences or tied up on the long-distance telephone.

It is on the telephone that you must catch editors, if you catch them at all, and then during the prime hours between ten and twelve in the morning and three and five in the afternoon—the very hours when they are most likely to be in meetings. (Many alleged meetings are simply invitations to get off the line.)

I have always found editors to be a rich source of gossip concerning happenings in the "trade." (They are almost as enlightening as garrulous secretaries, who are not always to be found.) To get the inside story on Publisher A, one has only to bide one's time until his editor has moved on to Publisher B. No one expects loyalty in this business to extend beyond one's place of current employment. It is for this reason that publishing has been called a goldfish bowl.

Writers, because most of them live at a distance from New York City, are the least likely targets for gossip. Only the very rich ones, like Norman Mailer, can afford to domicile near the jungle. To the question, "What is X like?"—the X being a client whom the editor has signed on—I always reply, "Your guess is as good as mine." When asked for a biographical sketch I explain that this may take a little time since I keep no such file in the office. An agent is usually more interested in what a client writes than in how he or she performs on the golf course or in bed.

Where do editors come from? The women seem to move up through the ranks, starting out as copy editors or editorial secretaries, while the men trickle in from eastern colleges, usually with the help of influential friends. But this is indeed only a trickle. Generally your concern will be finding out where the editor you worked with yesterday is employed today. They play this game of musical chairs pretty much in a closed society; thus, despite the constant movement from desk to desk and office to office, there always seems to be enough talent to go around. (Top executives also play musical chairs but, as the *New York Times* has pointed out, "only once in a blue moon do such job switches have much significance except to residents of Publishers' Row.")

Of course not all switches among editors are voluntary. There is an old saying in the business that when a firm is successful the publisher takes credit, and when it starts to slide the editor is not only held responsible but is usually relieved of a job. Firing is normally done in a very discreet manner; so that when one picks up *Publishers Weekly* and reads where so-and-so has decided to become a "free lancer," it is impossible to tell whether it was his or her own idea or the employer's. Query the latter and all you will learn is that the editor "is no longer with us"—a fact you are well aware of.

I remember when one of the large paperback houses had to

unload an important editor. The brass was in a quandary as to just how to go about it inoffensively. It was finally decided to let the word out that the gentleman had suffered a heart attack and was retiring for reasons of ill health. Nothing could have been farther from the truth, but for many months thereafter the poor man kept receiving solicitous inquiries about his health from concerned friends.

I sometimes amuse myself at luncheon by asking a particular editor what he or she is looking for. The reply is always the same: good books. When invited to define good books the answer is: books that will sell. And when asked what will sell the answer is always: good books.

Editors look for "good books" at lowest possible terms in order to impress their publishers with their frugality. Frequently they are given autonomy up to a certain level; ask for an advance above that level and they have to consult their boss. Many so-called acquisition editors pretend to have authority they do not possess unless it be to turn projects down. That is why you may receive a fast rejection from an editor but may have to wait weeks or even months for an acceptance.

Never tell an editor you have come up with an original idea, for there is no such thing. A substantial number of books published each year are deliberate spin-offs from previous successes, and no originality is intended. Editors study the sales figures of competitive houses and know when it is safe to offer the same thing again. This is called cashing in on a trend. Look at a hardcover bestseller list, and then go to your neighborhood paperback store and you will find imitations galore. Blockbuster movies are imitated in the same way.

To find anything original you would have to go back to the Old Testament, and even then it would be difficult. The stories of the Ark, of Jonah and the Whale, and of Daniel in the Lion's Den had earlier versions in other religious literature. The love story of Adam and Eve might have been original had it been written by Cain or Abel.

Never try to con an editor who has taken an interest in your work. Manuscripts speak for themselves. If a story has movie or TV possibilities, the editor will not need to be told by you. The less boasting you do the better. Editors know from experience that the writer who brags about a work invariably has nothing to offer.

There is nothing finer than a close understanding and friendship between author and editor, but it is always wise to let the latter make the first advances. By insisting upon too many personal meetings in the office, you can become expendable regardless of your talent. Remember, an editor's work is never done, and it behooves you not to make his or her life more difficult.

Many editors are frustrated writers. They may want to tinker with your manuscript. If they decide to rewrite a sentence occasionally, try to be tolerant. I have known editors to rewrite entire chapters of commercial novels with a view toward making them more readable. What does it matter unless you are turning out deathless prose? For all but a very few, writing is a business; any help that is likely to make your book more profitable should be gratefully accepted.

Whatever you may have read or heard about payola in publishing, *never* attempt to bribe an editor into selling you criticism. Never stick a check or a green bill into the envelope containing your manuscript. This has often been attempted, but I am sure it has always failed. No editor, no matter how hard up, will accept money from a stranger. Office time belongs to the employer. If you want to propose an outside-of-hours arrangement you have nothing to lose by trying, but you will probably be turned down. Such a request, if granted, would have to be on condition that said editor be under no obligation to consider your work for publication, and you would have to make this explicitly clear in your approach. I am sure some editors do moonlight to augment their incomes, but usually it is in the form of teaching classes and not in coaching individual writers.

Do editors read everything? I am sure that if it is the firm's policy to review the work of unagented writers then everything gets at least token consideration, even if only a page or two of copy are examined before rejection. An editor takes as much pride in discovering a talented new writer as that writer does in showing off a check for advance royalties. It is not to the credit of any editor to pass up talent which is later spotted by a competitor.

With writers coming and going, with good ones turning stale and old ones dying off, editors cannot afford to bank entirely upon their reservoir of familiar names. Each year a certain amount of new talent must emerge if there are to be big names for tomorrow's market. For this reason publishers gamble with first novels and editors are willing to assist a promising unknown in whipping a project into shape. A rigid diet of established reputations may eventually lead to starvation.

5

The Pantyhose Invasion

THERE HAVE ALWAYS BEEN WOMEN EDITORS IN PUBLISHING; WHEN I opted for a career in agenting, I took it for granted there would be one or two in every editorial office. But in those days, apart from magazines, they seemed to play an unimportant role.

Lois Dwight Cole of Macmillan was perhaps the best known woman editor in the hardcover field. Another well-known figure of the forties and fifties was Maria Leiper of Simon & Schuster, a charming, extremely bright lady whom I very much admired but never managed to sell to. (She had the three Bs: brains, beauty, and breeding.) Then there was Lee Wright, who made a name for herself in the mystery category. Henry Holt had a couple of imperishable ladies whose names I no longer remember. There were others. Magazines that appealed to women readers had women editors, but almost always the top executives were men.

It is not that way anymore. As this is being written, Fawcett and New American Library have women publishers. Dell, Avon, Pocket Books, and several smaller paperback houses have women in decision-making positions. This has come about because today the majority of book buyers are women, so that it makes sense that women should be allowed to select their fare.

A former sales manager of Fawcett Publications, Ed Lewis, once took me around the Florida Gold Coast area to show me the kind of display space he was getting for his firm's product. What surprised me as much as the excellent distribution of titles was the way the female customers in each store gathered around the books by women writers. Gothics, romances, romantic suspense, historicals—categories dominated by the so-called weaker sex—were the main attractions along with books on cooking and needlework.

A number of years ago, you may recall, there was a best-selling novel entitled *Rebecca* and another entitled *Forever Amber*. These books have served as models for the gothic and sexy historical of today. Women are now laboring successfully in both categories, writing books which are actually spin-offs from the originals. Why it took so long for these categories to become established is hard to say, unless one concludes that publishers are not very clairvoyant.

Modern gothics, following in the tradition of *Rebecca*, are moody, scary, and sexless. Modern historicals, following in the footsteps of *Forever Amber*, feature adventurous young ladies in dangerous and amorous situations. Back in the days of editor Harold Latham, the discoverer of *Gone With the Wind* and *How Green Was My Valley* and other famous Macmillan novels, sexy historicals were almost unheard of. Latham wrote in his memoirs that he was opposed to accepting *Forever Amber* because he felt it would hurt the firm to be identified with so much sex. Actually, by today's relaxed standards of morality, the Kathleen Winsor novel was innocuous. I wonder how Harold Latham would react to some of the more recent Avon historicals which have sold in the millions—mostly to women readers who love to read sexy novels if packaged by a reputable firm and not a porn factory.

In 1950 when the Fawcetts appeared on the scene with mass-market paperback fiction, there were so few women authors that I used to wonder why anyone bothered to employ women editors. Dick Carroll, the brain behind Gold Medal Books, explained it this way: "I guess they hire them because they come cheap." In the days before women's lib and equal rights for women, this may well have been the reason.

Publishing has become feminized to a startling degree. Many male editors, their egos bruised, are feeling very uncomfortable—like fish out of water. One confided to me recently that he was spending more than half his time reading women's fiction, of which he was admittedly no sure judge, where formerly he was preoccupied with hard-boiled suspense, male-oriented mysteries, and westerns. Another editor told me how painful it was to have to clear his recommendations with a lady publisher. Somehow he felt that his manhood was being threatened by having to play a subservient role in a house once known for its masculine product.

Will the pendulum ever swing back? I doubt it. During World War II, the Korean War, and the Vietnam War, men did a lot more reading and bought a lot more books than women. The PXs were filled with male-oriented material, for no soldier would be caught reading the kind of fiction women writers are grinding out today.

Consider the mystery category. At one time I had a large stable of male mystery writers who wrote tough stories with plenty of gore and as much sex as the times would tolerate. Peace brought a flood of English mysteries in which genteel victims would frequently be found slumped over a chess table or dying from a poison that had been slipped into their tea. Thus the Raymond Chandler school gave way to the school of Agatha Christie. When Hearst launched a line of paperbacks designed to revive the old Gold Medal type of masculine fiction, the results were disastrous and the effort was soon abandoned.

Nowadays publishers hire women editors not because they come cheap—which I suspect they do not—but because they know better than men what women like to read.

6

Payola

I MUST HAVE SPENT TWENTY-FIVE YEARS IN THE AGENCY BUSINESS before I learned about payola: the practice of paying for patronage. I knew it was customary at one time in the disc-jockey end of radio for record companies to sweeten the palms of the deejays in order to get certain records on the airwaves. It came as something of a surprise to me to learn that it was not unheard of for hungry or greedy editors to ask for, or to invite, payments under the table. So what do you do when an editor you consider a friend suggests he can buy a lot more of your clients' books if you are willing to slip him a little something on the side?

If you are a rat you can quietly report the editor to the publisher, and the editor will get the sack. If you are merely inclined to be smug just stop submitting anything in the future, and turn to other outlets. If you are a prig you will tell the editor off, mumble something about publishing being a gentleman's game—which means struggling to keep a straight face—and let the rascal seduce one of your competitors.

Certainly if there be a culprit in the payola business, it is the one who solicits and not the one who is approached. The solicitor does not always have to be the editor. I know one agent in town who has specialized in making improper advances. You buy my books, I will take care of you. Just like that. More than one agent has been thrown out of a publisher's office after having been caught in the act.

Agents make money; editors seldom do. I am much more sympathetically inclined toward a good but underpaid editor—usually a family man who works for some miserable niggard who denies the editor a living wage—than I am toward a grasping agent who scrounges around in the payola racket and jeopardizes an editor's position, just to make extra money that he or she does not really need.

I have always doubted that payola in the record business was ever as flagrant as the newspapers made it seem, or as wicked. There is *a priori* and *a posteriori* payola, by which I mean it is one thing to pay in advance to have a record promoted and another to offer a reward to a deejay for publicizing a good piece of music that might otherwise have been overlooked. I for one refuse to believe that the recipient of the latter gift is a criminal.

It was Norman Douglas who had one of his characters in *South Wind* say that "a conscience is a good slave but a bad master." Sometimes it is difficult to draw a sharp line between what is right and what is wrong. An agent's sole responsibility is to look after the interests of clients; so long as *they* do not get hurt, no sleep need be lost.

One runs into many temptations in dealing with underpaid editors. I have had a few, themselves one-time authors, offer me books to submit to their reprint firms that they have published under pen names with hardcover houses: in other words, to pass their own work through their own hands for consideration. What to do? If the books were dogs, they would not have been published in the first place. I take a pragmatic approach to this kind of situation. Instead of reading and assessing in my own mind the worthiness of the material, I trust in the integrity of the editor in each instance, and I count on the editor's respect for me as an agent not to involve me in what might amount to a rip-off.

Unfortunately not all editors worry about respectability. Some have been known to write copy suitable for their own publications and then sell it to themselves under pen names. A few years ago the editor of a leading hardcover firm accepted a kickback from an author who was a friend of his at the time; later the author turned on the editor, and the resulting bad publicity cost the latter his job. More recently a paperback editor, whose moral sense I had regarded as impeccable, was suddenly relieved of his post because of alleged shady dealings with a certain local agent, but not until after some pretty shoddy stuff had gone through the mill.

It is fair to say that the majority of editors, both men and women, are honest beyond a question of doubt. But as one of my old schoolteachers used to point out when he caught one of his students cheating on an exam: "There are a few rotten apples in every barrel." If the Creator had intended all men to be honest, He would have fashioned them that way—although it probably would have taken more than seven days.

PART FOUR

SOME
TYPICAL
MISCARRIAGES

*The following are condensed office reports
on projects in varying stages of development
that had either to be rejected or returned for revision.
Perhaps you will find your own faults pinpointed in a few of them.*

This project has possibilities, but the outline is much too skimpy for a serious work of nonfiction. The author says he can't take the time for research without a contract, and we can't get him a contract without giving the publisher a better idea of what he intends to do with each chapter.

*

There are too many books out on the same subject, and this one offers nothing new. Also dying is too serious a business to be treated humorously.

*

A good novella. But how can you sell 25,000 words these days when publishers are all looking for long books? It is much too sexy for the women's magazines.

*

It has the makings of a salable novel. But if it is to be a saga, two generations are hardly enough. Also there is too much shifting around of viewpoint. Three generations, each seen from the viewpoint of a female character, should do it. Let's get this one back again.

*

Excellent local color but no conflict between hero and heroine. They meet, fall in love in the middle of the book and the rest is anticlimactic. There must be an obstacle that comes between them and threatens their relationship. It's worth seeing again if only because of the excellent color and clean composition.

*

It's all history and no romance. A smattering of history is sufficient for a period love story. Can't be salvaged.

*

Novels in letter form are almost impossible to sell. This is not convincing. The letters all read as if written by the same person when supposedly they have been written by a man to a woman and vice versa. Looks pretty hopeless.

*

The problem here is the multiple viewpoint in what is really a one-viewpoint story. The whole novel can be written through the eyes of the lead character who has the only real problem. Also there is much too much yak. Not worth seeing again.

*

This purports to be a literary novel. It is slice-of-life, with no semblance of plot, and the slices are cut much too thin. Also the composition is too pedestrian for a literary novel in the first place. The narrator is well characterized, but the other characters are mere names.

*

The outline suggests that this is going to be written from the wrong character's viewpoint. Lila has the vital problem in the story, and the focal character obviously has not. It needs recasting.

*

This outline should be put on ice for the present. There have been too many books recently about the KKK.

*

There are two principal characters, and the book jumps back and forth from one to the other. The author must decide which one to put in focus.

*

This story starts too soon. It should open with the girl already in Cairo and then flash back to the Boston scene briefly. The first fifty pages can be boiled down to a few paragraphs.

*

A good, tough adventure story, but the first two chapters are so complicated that no reader could plow through them. Some of the early information can be given to the reader a little at a time as the story progresses—perhaps in dialogue. There are too many long paragraphs. Who does he think he is: Marcel Proust? Worth another look.

*

For a novel this has too many long descriptions. It would make a good travel guide, but there's not enough story development to hold the reader's interest.

*

This has the makings of a good mystery, but it needs more suspects. As it is the villain is too easy to spot. I had the puzzle solved by page 50. The clues are a little too transparent. Worth developing because of the unusual setting.

*

The story line is okay, but the heroine should be at the center of the action. As it is the action moves around her, and she is only remotely involved. Has good style and authentic background. Worth having revised. But not on onionskin paper! Too hard on the eyes.

*

The composition here is much too loose. Whole paragraphs can be thrown out, and at least one chapter (4) is completely superfluous. The author writes as if he were being paid by the word.

*

This is probably salable. Almost anything in the self-help area has a market these days. But let's get a professionally typed script. No one wants to read 250 pages of faded type. I had to read it in a bright light!

*

Here is a romance with no romance. The entire first half of the book seems to be about horticulture. Maybe the author should switch to nonfiction. It would interest rose fanciers but not housewives in search of vicarious trysts in the moonlight. Not salable.

*

Not a smart idea in a mystery to have a cardinal turn out to be the murderer. What would Catholic readers think?

*

The heroine is not sympathetic, so who cares about her problems? This one would never go.

*

Too much historical material and not enough current fact about flying saucers. UFO addicts are more interested in recent sightings than in the fireball Moses thought he saw in the sky. Book is too dull. UFO books must be more entertaining and a little frightening besides.

*

The writer obviously knows Amsterdam night life, and this could be a good bet for armchair swingers. But the writing is too cute. It would turn off sophisticated readers. Needs redrafting.

*

This gothic is on the dull side. The heroine herself is never in danger. She seems more interested in food and clothes and small-town society than in finding out what's going on around her. Don't see how this can be saved.

*

A good exposé of regional political scandals, but market much too limited. I don't know who would buy it outside the author's immediate area. Well written. Too bad.

*

To sell a book on animal navigation you have to have the necessary credentials. This is an excellent blueprint, and I am sure it would make a readable book. But you'd need a better label for the can.

*

It's a fascinating documentary, but it's libelous. No publisher would touch it.

*

It takes four to six months to put out a book. By the time this one could come out the material would be dated. Maybe a newspaper would buy it.

*

This reads like a converted screenplay. All talk and no atmosphere or characterization. Wouldn't stand a chance.

*

The plotting is okay but the composition is deadwood. The writer probably needs more vitamins.

*

This will sell, but the first chapter is from the viewpoint of a minor character and this should not be. There is no reason why the hero can't be on stage from the start. Otherwise okay.

*

The graphic sex scenes in this one are quite visual, but they are presented in language that is much too crude. Maybe the lady can make the writing a little more sensitive and not so much like the kind of prose you find in pornographic bookshops. Because of the barroom lingo, I didn't find the sex scenes very titillating. Worth revising.

*

Beautiful writing, but the story is too sordid and too depressing for light romance. Readers of these books want to escape from the very realities that she is writing about. We can try, but I don't think it will go.

*

In an adventure story the action should be well spaced. Here it all comes in the first half of the novel. After page 150 the reader would fall asleep!

*

This outline is much too skimpy for a 200,000-word historical romance. An editor would have to see a fuller blueprint.

*

This is a romance written in the first person by a male whose lady characters, from the narrator on down, all talk like himself. In the third person the macho dialogue might not be so noticeable; but even with a viewpoint change, the talk would have to be toned down and individualized.

*

A woman's novel with a racing car background. I doubt if it would go. The setting is too gutsy for sweet romance.

*

This writer is a born storyteller, but the composition is so rough that it's hard to follow the action. It would drive a copy editor up the wall. Maybe she knows an English teacher who could help her put her sentences in shape.

*

An attempt at an erotic historical. The sex scenes are graphic enough, and the writer is uninhibited. But the scenes are too abrupt—usually confined to a paragraph or two. If the writer expects to titillate the reader, she should stretch them out more. There should be some foreplay so you don't get the feeling you're watching a couple of monkeys in the zoo.

*

The original narrator is killed off on page 40, and a new narrator takes over. Good writing, but amateurish technique. The book should begin on page 40.

*

Too much editorializing. Nobody cares what the writer thinks about political conventions. Who's he? The book should stick to telling what goes on. The facts presented are entertaining and illuminating, and there is evidence of careful research.

*

The lead characters are too old for sweet romance. They look a little ridiculous fumbling around in the moonlight. Maybe the writer could salvage the plot and throw out the antique lovers. Okay for the hero to be graying at the temples, but the heroine should not be over 35, even if she *has* gone through two previous husbands.

*

A multiple-viewpoint novel that has gotten out of hand. The character at the start, with whom we are supposed to identify, is out of the story too much: once for about fifty pages, another time for thirty-five. Since he's the only character that anybody but an idiot would want to identify with, the book sags without him.

*

This is a whitewash of the insurance racket. The writer should get it subsidized by Travelers. No publisher would buy it.

*

Needs a dozen before-and-after illustrations. The author has the credentials, and there is always a market for a book on plastic surgery. But the reader would like to *see* what kind of job the author performs on his patients and not just hear tell about it. Self-serving, but interesting. Let's get pix.

*

Humor is too hard to sell, and the humor here is sporadic. It would need a lot more doing to be salable.

*

PART FIVE

QUESTIONS
AND ANSWERS

*The following questions
are among those most frequently put to me by interviewers,
students, and professional writers.*

QUESTION: *Is it true that agents hate writers?*

ANSWER: Let's put it this way: some writers are difficult to love. It is not really a matter of hating. It so happens that I am not especially fond of liquor. However, were I willing to put up with the kind of abuse some agents take from their clients, I am sure I would become an alcoholic.

Writers *have* driven agents to drink. How? There are many ways. They can write long letters—several pages single-spaced—full of questions that have to be answered; they can ask about an allegedly missing payment which the agent must take time to track down in the checkbook and show proof of by having the endorsed check photostated and sent on; they can start asking about the editor's opinion of a script that has been in the editor's office for only a few days; they can give the agent instructions as to where a manuscript or an outline should be sent, how much it should be worth, and how long it should take the editor to issue a check for its purchase; or they can tell the agent how much more money a friend is making on the same kind of book with the very same publisher and suggest that something should be done about renegotiating the contract.

A special kind of torture involves the middle-of-night telephone call—especially if it comes from the West Coast when it is dinnertime in California and bedtime in New York. I have often been awakened from pleasant dreams to be told that I need a new representative in Beverly Hills because the old one has failed to sell movie rights to a pet opus. On such occasions I count the hours before I can get to the office and write a farewell letter.

Agents who handle local talent are the most put upon; happily, I do not. I once had occasion to call on a competitor during office hours. His reception room was full of hungry-looking writers of both sexes sitting with manuscripts on their laps and awaiting the opportunity to talk up their brain children. I seldom let a local writer into my office. One of the smartest agents in the business, whose name I will not bother advertising, eats sandwiches at his desk, seldom raps with his clients, and conducts all his business on the telephone.

No discussion of how to torture a mild-mannered literary agent would be complete without some reference to the business of borrowing money. I used to run a kind of loan association for my clients in order to hold them in line. Today I avoid the hungry account. The fact that only 2 percent of the writers in America earn their living entirely with a pen is one that I never let escape my mind. The writer with several kids to support is a very bad risk for my agency. I will settle any day of the week for a less talented client who manages to stay solvent without borrowing money.

*

QUESTION: *What advice do you have to offer a young novelist?*

ANSWER: I am a salesman and not a teacher of writing. However, I think it important for a novelist to learn basics.

I often suggest to young novelists that they sit down at a piano and stretch one hand over an octave. Each letter in that octave represents an ingredient essential to good fiction:

C—*characterization*
D—*dialogue*
E—*entertainment*
F—*friction*
G—*genre*
A—*action*
B—*background*
C—*composition*

Failure to give careful attention to any one of these ingredients can result in an unsalable novel.

Characterization. There is more to this than creating a number of believable men and women. To gain a reader's interest, there must be a character with whom the reader can readily identify, and this character is usually sympathetically drawn. Antiheroes and antiheroines exist in popular fiction, but they are greatly outnumbered by heroes and heroines the reader would like to know and take home to dinner. Characters must be allowed to talk, and their talk must be individualized so that they do not sound as if they were all speaking through the mouth of the author.

Dialogue. It is what gives a novel buoyancy. Long pages of narration and exposition will quickly turn a reader off. On the other hand, an excess of dialogue will make a book read like a novelized screenplay. (The chief objection to novelized screenplays is too much yak and not enough character development.)

Entertainment. A novel must be engaging. Boring people too often turn out boring novels. A writer who has charisma is likely to inject some of it into the printed word. A writer with a message to deliver is inclined to forget that a novelist's job is to entertain.

Friction. This is synonymous with conflict. Things must go wrong. The sympathetic hero or heroine must get into deeper and deeper difficulty in trying to solve his or her problem. There must be a steady build-up of friction if the novel is to avoid a letdown. This requires a careful ordering of scenes so that tension is sustained. Some writers put their important scenes on index cards so that they can be arranged in a way which will not result in an anticlimax.

Genre. An element important in commercial fiction because there is a reluctance on the part of editors to mix up categories. True, there have been nurse gothics, erotic historicals, romantic westerns. But a writer should not undertake to mix categories without some encouragement from an editor who wishes to experiment with something different. Occasionally a mixed category becomes a new category in itself: thus the erotic historical, a mixture of sex and history, which in recent years has become very popular. I have had romances rejected because they contain elements of mystery and gothics turned down because of nurse heroines.

Action. A necessity in the commercial novel. Endless discussions, with the characters sitting around a fireside, are a no-no. Solid pages of description are a turn-off. An otherwise readable romance may be rejected because the author devotes too much space to describing the hero's occupation, meanwhile letting the story stand still. Furthermore, action must advance the plot toward the inevitable climax and must not just feature the characters moving about aimlessly.

Background. Something every good novel must have so it does not take place in a void. The reader must be allowed to visualize the scenes, even if the setting is imaginary and does not represent an actual place on the planet. Sometimes a particularly exotic background will carry a borderline story into print. It has happened in my office time and again. One paperback house that has achieved enormous success with this formula is Harlequin Books of Canada. This firm lays great emphasis upon unusual locales that offer armchair travelers a satisfactory means of escaping their humdrum surroundings.

Composition. This refers to the style of your manuscript. A strong writer—meaning one who has a fine command of the language, who punctuates properly, and uses correct grammar—almost always makes out. Conversely, a wobbly writer must depend more upon plotting. It is a fact, as every agent and editor knows, that strong composition and strong plot sense do not often go together. The best stylists are usually the worst plotters, and the best storytellers are usually the ones who give copy editors nightmares.

Here, then, are eight elements of importance in the writing of a popular novel. How to give each the proper amount of attention is the novelist's business and not mine. My business is to be sure that none of those elements is neglected before sending the product to market.

*

QUESTION: *How should I prepare an outline for a nonfiction book?*

ANSWER: There is no hard-and-fast rule that I know of when it comes to outlining a nonfiction project. In my office, I refer to *tables of contents* rather than outlines, for I think this gives the writer a better picture of what I would like to send to market.

A typical table of contents would provide individual chapter headings and would offer a brief summary of what is going to go into each chapter. In this way it is easier for an agent, or an editor, to juggle chapters around, perhaps eliminate one, or ask for a fuller summary of another.

The summary can be in the form of a solid paragraph or several paragraphs if required. However, I much prefer the use of disconnected phrases, separated by a series of dashes. Again, this makes it possible for an editor to delete an idea or request that another section of the chapter be expanded.

As an illustration I have chosen a nonfiction book at random and have opened to the page called CONTENTS. Roman numerals identify the chapters, and each chapter has its own heading. Chapter V concerns the Etruscan Countryside:

Fertility of the land — The problem of malaria — The success of
Etruscan hydraulics — The right of property — The cereals — Vines
and trees — Agricultural implements — Hunting — Fishing — The
timber industry — The mines — The roads — The vehicles

The particular book from which the above was chosen also
happens to have an index. That, however, is for the publisher to
decide.

*

QUESTION: *Granted that most writers are difficult to deal with, which ones are
the most troublesome?*

ANSWER: The most troublesome, for me, are the ones that have venal
tendencies. I am not thinking so much of the plagiarists or the
hoaxsters like Clifford Irving, or even of the short-change artists
who sign up for 100,000 words and end up 20,000 to 30,000 words
short. Nor am I thinking of the willful option-breakers who always have some stinker ready to serve up to a publisher they are
trying to ditch. Even writers who contract to perform exclusively
for one firm and sneak out projects for a competitor under a pen
name can justify such actions, if prolific enough to turn out more
copy than one publisher can handle.

The real menace, I think, is the writer who cons a publisher into
issuing a contract and a portion of an advance and then makes no
attempt to deliver. Why publishers are so tolerant of this kind of
rip-off has always puzzled me. Is it that they are afraid of alienat-
ing such a writer and, if so, why should they care? Is it that they
hesitate to take legal action against such thievery because they
consider it demeaning to garnishee a salary or put a culprit in jail?

For an agent, this literary con man is an ever-present threat, and
the more reputable the agent the greater is the danger of becoming involved. The rascal has only to turn out a promising outline
on a surefire subject, offer it to a middleman whom publishers respect, then sit back and wait for a deal.

I have been fooled many times by these tricksters and have yet
to discover a foolproof defense. It is regrettable that the more
successful they are in getting away with it the bolder they become. A crooked writer can almost make a living pocketing advances on work that he or she never intends to produce.

*

QUESTION: *Are men or are women easier to work with?*

ANSWER: Women, by far. When I started in business, most commercial writers were men. Today, while most top-money writers are still men, the editorial emphasis has shifted to the other sex. It has been estimated that well over 60 percent of all retail book purchases are made by women, and women prefer to read books by women. This is especially true of fiction.

How do I feel about the new emphasis? I like it fine. Only one woman writer has ever given me the shaft, whereas I have lost male clients for a variety of reasons: I am too abrasive, too critical of what is sent in; I fail to lend them money; or I fail to negotiate contracts that do justice to their talent. I lost a writer once because he felt I was making him into a literary whore. I lost another because he did not like my politics.

I have no idea how it is with the truly literary female writers, for those I avoid like lepers. I must confess I have heard horrendous stories of hysterical women and their temper tantrums at the sight of a discouraging royalty statement, but I have had no personal experiences of this kind.

Today I enjoy good relations with my male clients because I take pains to weed out the alcoholics, the crybabies, and the panhandlers. Still, I am much happier representing women. I find them more loyal, patient, and understanding. Rarely will they venture to borrow money, and seldom will they "forget" to return it if they do.

When a lady client complains, it is usually with justification. Imaginary grievances are virtually unknown. Through inexcusable negligence I once allowed a paperback publisher to go nine weeks before mailing me a contract on a book that his editor had accepted for publication. At the end of the nine weeks I got a polite note from the author suggesting that maybe the editor had changed his mind and that I should offer the work elsewhere. A man in a similar situation would have blown his fuse.

It is true that the financial status of married women writers often permits a more cavalier attitude toward money. Many husbands are good providers. But there are plenty of single women and widows writing books these days who are partly or wholly dependent upon their earnings.

When it comes to meeting deadlines, a woman is more reliable. If her husband is ill or if one of the kids is having surgery, naturally she must ask for an extension. But she is not likely to wait until the script is overdue and probably on the publisher's schedule before requesting more time.

I have mentioned elsewhere the male writers who take advances, spend them, and then fail to deliver. Yet in all my years as an agent I have never encountered a single such experience with a woman writer. They are not likely to squander their advance on a binge, a new sports car, or a love affair and then complain that they cannot afford to write the book because the money has already been spent.

Correspondence with lady writers is usually more cordial and often more entertaining than are written exchanges with men. Their letters generally reveal a better sense of humor, and they have a way of glossing over personal problems. Most crybabies I have dealt with have been men, for men are much more inclined to dramatize their financial predicaments, slander their misunderstood mates, and inveigh against the stupidity of editors who offer what is intended to be helpful criticism. Women, on the other hand, are usually more receptive to criticism. Dissect the work of a male client and you are asking for trouble. Women have more humility and are even capable of expressing gratitude when their shortcomings are pointed out to them.

It is the sheer gratitude of women writers when you do a good job of handling their accounts that overwhelms me. Over the years several of them have seen fit to will me their literary estates; a total to date of over 300 properties. No male client has ever willed me so much as a wooden nickel.

I believe that the recent emancipation of women and the work of writers such as Jacqueline Susann, Erica Jong, Gael Greene, Joyce Haber, and others who have written intimately and honestly about women's sexual experiences have done much to bring the lady writer out of her shell. Avon, with its million-copy sellers by unknown housewives willing to develop explicit sex scenes in their historical novels, deserves high marks among paperback publishers for pioneering a new course for women's fiction.

Writing, believe me, is only big business for a chosen few. Actually it is hard today for the average male writer to earn enough at the typewriter to support a family. For this reason, I suppose the greater degree of hard-headedness among male writers is understandable.

*

QUESTION: *Is there any chance of selling behind the Iron Curtain in the foreseeable future?*

ANSWER: Every New York agent worth his salt has affiliates in important foreign capitals. In some countries, notably France, Germany, Italy, and Holland, these affiliates can produce substantial revenue for the writers. In others, such as Spain, Portugal, Greece, Turkey, and the countries of South America, possibilities are limited because of poverty or illiteracy or both.

Behind the Iron Curtain the situation is almost hopeless, and many agents make no effort to get sales. I will never forget the astonished expression on the face of the young lady in Budapest, who manages the state-controlled literary agency, when I offered to send her samples of commercial fiction. "But this sort of thing," she protested, "is trash suitable only for western democracies. In Hungary we try to educate our people to read classics. The last thing we want is to pollute their minds with that kind of material."

I had received a similar reception in Belgrade the year before when I chatted with the government agent. The Yugoslavs, as everyone knows, enjoy more freedom than any of the other Iron Curtain countries. Still the policy is to discourage popular fiction. When I mentioned that I controlled over a thousand commercial properties, either as owner or owners' representative, I was instructed to submit "one sample in each category." It was a polite way of telling me to get lost.

*

QUESTION: *What special tax deductions is a writer entitled to?*
ANSWER: To qualify for deductions, you must establish yourself as a professional writer. This means that you must be able to show either a contract for publication of a book, a firm commitment from a magazine for the purchase of material, or samples of published work in book or magazine form. You cannot claim deductions of any kind if you are unpublished; and in the magazine field the IRS will take a dim view of your professional standing if all you have to show are sample articles, poems, or stories printed in so-called little magazines that do not pay in hard cold cash.

It is not necessary for you to write full-time in order to qualify as a professional. You may hold other jobs in the daytime and do all your writing nights and weekends. But you must have evidence of success in your endeavors, and it would be a very good idea for the credit side of your ledger to show a larger figure than the debit. If you invest heavily in researching work for a limited and low-paying market, so that your losses substantially exceed your profits at the end of the year, then your position, taxwise, is insecure.

You may ask if there are there people who turn to writing as a means of beating the tax rap. This I very much doubt. It would not make sense to rent office space, hire a secretary or stenographer, buy office equipment, and pay for heat and electricity unless a writer had reason to believe that income would be sufficient to justify the outlay. The IRS computers would soon pick out your return if it became obvious you were deliberately engaged in recording an annual loss.

My advice to "professional" writers who constantly operate in the red and who deduct travel and hotel expenses far in excess of earnings is, *Don't.* You are certain to be singled out for audit. Even highly successful authors are frequently audited because of legitimate travel expenses incurred in connection with their research. The least you can do is keep out of the red ink.

Obviously the writer who is assigned to turn out books or articles about places or things is more justified in running up travel and entertainment expenses than is the novelist who researches out of the neighborhood library or the poet or playwright who draws from imagination. Common sense will keep you out of messy situations with the IRS. It might be a good idea for you to play devil's advocate and, in looking over your planned tax deductions, ask whether you, if you were examining them, would consider them legitimate.

Until recently a professional writer was permitted to deduct a portion of the house rent or the monthly mortgage payment from taxable income. If the den of a nine room house was used as an office, then one-ninth of these expenses could be considered tax deductible. Unfortunately this privilege no longer obtains; you must use the space exclusively as an office in order to qualify.

If you rent a special office for your writing, all expenses you then incur will be considered deductible: furniture can be amortized, along with typewriter, dictating machine, copier, or whatever. Heat and electricity costs, if you pay them and can show proof, can be taken off your tax bite. Repairs, decorating, cleaning, and, of course, office help are legitimate deductions.

If you do not have exclusive office space, your deductions will be limited to business postage, phone calls, ribbons, tapes, paper, photographic film, and typewriter upkeep expenses. Yes, you can still amortize the cost of your electric typewriter, and you can deduct for secretarial or stenographic help. But you must have bills for everything in case you are audited. Your writing expenses may be quite legitimate, but your tax return may be singled out for some quite different reason, such as excessive charity or medical deductions, for example, or faulty arithmetic.

Writers who must travel on special assignment should keep day-to-day diaries of all expenses. Although membership in various writers' organizations constitutes a legitimate expense, travel to their meetings—which may be half a continent or more away—is likely to be questioned and disallowed. Even an IRS inspector who knows nothing about the publishing business is not likely to be stupid enough to believe that a mystery writer living in Kansas City must travel to New York to attend the annual MWA dinner. Similarly, a writer who lives in Boston is not likely to get away with a summer visit to a writers' conference in Seattle. These are risky deductions that invite scrutiny.

Among other legitimate deductions are the following: books and magazines that are useful in furthering your career as a writer, copyright fees, encyclopedias, dictionaries, fees for Xeroxing your manuscripts in lieu of making carbon copies, and last but not least the fees of a professional accountant.

*

QUESTION: *Do you believe that writing can be taught?*

ANSWER: You can be taught basics, but nobody can teach you how to acquire talent. Most of the energy expended by teachers of writing is wasted for this reason. If you want to be a composer you can study for years, master all the various keys, learn to run chords and arpeggios, become an accomplished student of harmony, but if you have no creative ability you are never going to compose anything worth listening to. The same is true of writing.

In college I took numerous courses in composition. I learned to punctuate, when to start a new paragraph, how to become conscious of clichés, omnibus sentences, purple passages, and dangling participles. The professors always demonstrated weaknesses by reading bad examples in class. If a singularly well-ordered opus was turned in and read aloud to the students, nothing so vulgar as its commercial value was ever discussed. It did not occur to any of these instructors of youth to suggest that if you wanted to write, say, for the magazines, you should single out the ones that published the kind of thing that interested you and *slant*. No one was ever told about length requirements, taboos, readership, and the like. To discuss the amount of money a periodical was likely to pay for an acceptance was unthinkable. Most of these courses still take place in a vacuum, so that even today a writer of talent, should such a one exist in a college classroom, would leave the course no wiser than before.

Adult courses in writing are generally of a more practical nature, and some attention *is* paid to the business side of the profession. Unfortunately you will rarely find anything resembling talent in attendance. I conducted courses for three years, both in Cambridge and New York, and had an opportunity to study the grown men and women who are drawn to them. Mostly they are bored housewives and tired businessmen who have fantasized themselves into believing they can become writers. They might just as well have signed up for the courses in weather forecasting or home economics that were being given down the hall.

Summer conferences for writers, except for Bread Loaf and one or two others, offer pleasant vacation retreats and an opportunity to mingle with agents and honest-to-God authors who also like to get away from their jungle habitats in the big cities. I was the agent-in-residence some years back at one of these. The original invitation was irresistible, "We are quite close to the mountains and the sea and have excellent golf courses and tennis courts in the vicinity." No mention was made of the quality of the enrollees upon whom one was to shower one's words of wisdom.

A talented writer usually knows enough to stay clear of books on how to write, of college writing courses, of adult-education classes, and of summer conferences. But even if a talented writer does not, the gift that he or she possesses is not likely to benefit the less fortunate. For this reason I have always advised young writers to keep company with bricklayers, used-car salesmen, prostitutes, department-store buyers—in fact almost anybody whose experience may brush off on them and broaden their knowledge of life—but to stay away from other writers.

*

QUESTION: *What books and magazines do you recommend for a writer's library?*

ANSWER: The most important, if you can afford it, is the *Encyclopaedia Brittanica*, but if you are short of space you can make do with the one-volume *Columbia Encyclopedia*. A copy of *Webster's Collegiate Dictionary* will also serve you well, but the *American Heritage Dictionary* would be a suitable alternative.

The *Rand McNally Atlas* is useful in checking place names and how these names are spelled. *Webster's Geographical Dictionary* is also helpful, containing as it does more than 40,000 geographic locations with notes about each one.

For the writer who has trouble with English, Fowler's *A Dictionary of Modern English Usage* will teach you the difference between *will* and *shall* and similar subtleties. I wish hotels, instead of sticking a Bible in every room, would switch to the Fowler book—which should be studied by everyone who attempts to use correct English and should be stuffed down the throats of all radio and TV announcers.

Roget's Thesaurus, a classical dictionary for writers in search of synonyms, is also a must for your library; and if you are writing nonfiction, I would also suggest a copy of *Bartlett's Familiar Quotations*. Many writers and most public speakers are acquainted with this one and can impress their readers and listeners with their erudition even if they have never read a single work from which the quotations have been extracted.

Bowker's *Literary Market Place* and *Publishers Weekly* have already been mentioned. The Sunday *New York Times*, which has recently been redesigned to be more readable, would be worth subscribing to for its book review section, as would either *Time* or *Newsweek*. If you have a public library within walking or comfortable driving distance from your home, the above shouldgive you adequate sources. Fiction writers, however, may find the *National Geographic* one additional publication that can provide exotic background material for their stories and novels.

*

QUESTION: *What is a writer's obligation concerning photographs for a work of nonfiction?*

ANSWER: Illustrations can make or break the sale of a nonfiction book and are therefore very important. If your illustrations are of inferior quality and there is nothing you can do about it, your text is liable to be rejected. If you insist upon the inclusion of an excessive number of illustrations—a number sufficient to place the retail cost out of reach—your text may also be turned down. On the other hand, fantastic illustrations can sometimes pull a weak text through.

It costs many times more to produce an illustration than it does a page of type, and I am talking about photographs in black and white. As for color, unless you are signed to produce a coffee-table book that is to sell for from $25 to $50, you may have to settle for one colorplate in the front of your book, or for none at all.

A book that requires photographs may accommodate as many as 16 plates. If a publisher uses 24, 32, or 48, he can expect to lose thousands of potential buyers because his retail price will be too high. Many writers fail to appreciate the cost of illustrations, and many readers fail to understand why they must be asked to pay seemingly outlandish prices for heavily illustrated nonfiction books. Line illustrations, however, are a different matter. These can be produced inexpensively and are often used to decorate even works of fiction, which certainly do not require them.

Writers should leave the problem of illustrations up to the publisher and not jeopardize a sale by making unreasonable demands. Be satisfied with one colorplate, since four colorplates mixed in with a number of black-and-white illustrations only call the buyer's attention to the dearth of color generally. If you buy an art book at a museum and find only four colorplates, you feel deprived. But if you find only black-and-white throughout, you may not be upset to find color missing. Books made up entirely of colorplates are invariably international arrangements where several foreign houses pool costs and insure a wide distribution. For a book calculated to sell only 5,000 to 10,000 copies color is not practical, except on the jacket. (You may be able to persuade a publisher to use the jacket illustration for the frontispiece inside.)

It is the writer's job to provide illustrations and usually the publisher's responsibility to pay for printing them. Illustrated texts usually mean a slight decrease in the sliding royalty: perhaps 10 percent to the first 10,000 copies sold instead of 10 percent to 5,000. Some publishers will try to pay royalties on wholesale instead of on retail if the cost of illustrating a book is very high.

The author must also indemnify the publisher in case of any copyright infringement involving the illustrations. There are agencies you can turn to for help in this area, and their fees are nominal. By using an agency, you relieve yourself of any copyright responsibility. Just remember photographs are protected by copyright the same as books, and there are penalties for mistaking a photograph that is under copyright protection for one you think is in public domain. (Under the old copyright law, the same 28-plus-28-year conditions remain and apply to all photographs taken prior to the change in the law.)

There are situations in which the cost of photography is borne by the publisher, but you must never count on such good fortune. As manufacturing costs rise, fewer firms are likely to be willing to foot your bill. Obviously if a firm wants a property badly enough, and if the author is indigent and unable to provide suitable illustrations, it may take on the financial responsibility. But more likely you will find that the cost has been deducted from your semiannual royalty statement—along with the cost of preparing the index which you have failed to provide and the cost of excessive fiddling with the proofs!

*

QUESTION: *What advice do you have for free-lance article writers?*

ANSWER: It can be simply stated. Slant carefully for particular periodicals, and never write an article unless an editor has offered you some encouragement. Many writers decide to write an article and proceed to turn it out on speculation, without even considering where it is to go when completed. Some work with an alphabetical list of periodicals and go right down the line, wasting postage as well as editors' time. Then they wonder why they receive so many rejection slips.

It would be a good idea not to spread out in too many directions. There are areas in which you can specialize without an advanced degree. If an editor can identify your name with a particular subject area, you may find yourself receiving assignments where otherwise you would have to make all the approaches.

Go to a well-stocked newsstand, or better still to a public library, where you can browse among the many types of magazines. Take notes on their contents, the length and tone of their articles, the reputations of their contributors. When you have selected a few that seem right for you, work up two or three ideas and submit them to the editors. It will not take an editor much longer to look at two or three ideas than it would to look at just one, and this will reduce the amount of correspondence. *Always* enclose a self-addressed stamped envelope, and do not mention previous sales to publications that an editor might be unimpressed with. (There are only about a dozen magazines in the country where an acceptance is worth bragging about.)

Sometimes a magazine will give you a small advance which you're entitled to keep if the completed article is turned down. However, if you are unknown, you will most likely be asked to write the entire piece on speculation.

When you sell an article, try to reserve all but the first serial rights. Reputable firms that insist upon acquiring all rights will either assign secondary rights back to you after publication or else will arrange to have you share in any subsidiary sales, such as to *Reader's Digest* or to magazines published abroad.

The two words for you to always bear in mind are *slant* and *query*. Otherwise you may be wasting your time and the time of a busy editor who has a pile of rejection slips in the drawer of his desk.

*

QUESTION: *If a book is rejected because of poor composition, how does one go about cleaning it up?*

ANSWER: I once prepared a checklist of stylistic pitfalls as follows:

> trite expressions
> clichés
> tiresome inversions
> dangling participles
> thin paragraphing
> long, heavy paragraphing
> no paragraphing at all
> excessive use of similes
> mixed metaphors
> unintentional alliteration
> rough cadences
> words used improperly
> word repetitions within a sentence
> purple passages intended to be beautiful
> rhyming words
> omnibus sentences
> uncommon words
> stilted phraseology
> superfluous punctuation
> too many adjectives
> redundancies
> circumlocutions
> introductory adverbs
> poor continuity of sentences
> capitalizations that shouldn't be
> misspelling of simple words

Index